The Early Modern Englishwoman:
A Facsimile Library of Essential Works

Series II

Printed Writings, 1641–1700: Part 2

Volume 1

An Collins

Introduced by
Robert C. Evans

General Editors
Betty S. Travitsky and Anne Lake Prescott

The Introductory Note copyright © Robert C. Evans 2003

Published by
Ashgate Publishing Limited
Gower House
Croft Road
Aldershot
Hants GU11 3HR
England

Ashgate Publishing Company
Suite 420
101 Cherry Street
Burlington, VT 05401–4405
USA

Ashgate website: http://www.ashgate.com

British Library Cataloguing-in-Publication Data
Collins, An, 17th cent.
   An Collins. - (The early modern Englishwoman : a facsimile
   library of essential works. Printed writings 1641-1700,
   series 2 ; pt. 2, v. 1)
   1.Devotional poetry, English
   I.Title II.Evans, Robert C.
   821.4

Library of Congress Cataloging-in-Publication Data
The early modern Englishwoman: a facsimile library of essential works. Part 1.
Printed Writings 1641–1700 / general editors, Betty S. Travitsky and Anne Lake
Prescott.

Library of Congress Control Number: 2003100275

The image reproduced on the title page and on the case is taken from the frontispiece portrait in *Poems, By the Most Deservedly Admired Mrs. Katherine Philips* (1667). Reproduced by permission of the Folger Shakespeare Library, Washington, DC.

ISBN 0 7546 3093 5

Printed in Great Britain by Antony Rowe Ltd, Chippenham, Wiltshire.

CONTENTS

PREFACE
BY THE GENERAL EDITORS

Until very recently, scholars of the early modern period have assumed that there were no Judith Shakespeares in early modern England. Much of the energy of the current generation of scholars has been devoted to constructing a history of early modern England that takes into account what women actually wrote, what women actually read, and what women actually did. In so doing the masculinist representation of early modern women, both in their own time and ours, is deconstructed. The study of early modern women has thus become one of the most important—indeed perhaps the most important—means for the rewriting of early modern history.

The Early Modern Englishwoman: A Facsimile Library of Essential Works is one of the developments of this energetic reappraisal of the period. As the names on our advisory board and our list of editors testify, it has been the beneficiary of scholarship in the field, and we hope it will also be an essential part of that scholarship's continuing momentum.

The Early Modern Englishwoman is designed to make available a comprehensive and focused collection of writings in English from 1500 to 1750, both by women and for and about them. The three series of *Printed Writings* (1500–1640, 1641–1700, and 1701–1750) provide a comprehensive if not entirely complete collection of the separately published writings by women. In reprinting these writings we intend to remedy one of the major obstacles to the advancement of feminist criticism of the early modern period, namely the limited availability of the very texts upon which the field is based. The volumes in the facsimile library reproduce carefully chosen copies of these texts, incorporating significant variants (usually in appendices). Each text is preceded by a short introduction providing an overview of the life and work of a writer along with a survey of important scholarship. These works, we strongly believe, deserve a large readership—of historians, literary critics, feminist critics, and non-specialist readers.

The Early Modern Englishwoman also includes separate facsimile series of *Essential Works for the Study of Early Modern Women* and of *Manuscript Writings*. These facsimile series are complemented by *The Early Modern Englishwoman 1500–1750: Contemporary Editions*. Also under our general editorship, this series will include both old-spelling and modernized editions of works by and about women and gender in early modern England.

New York City
2003

INTRODUCTORY NOTE

The precise identity of 'An Collins' remains a mystery. Stanley Stewart long ago raised (although he did not endorse) the possibility that her printed name might be a pseudonym (Stewart, p. ii), and he also mentioned that even if a person by such a name really *did* exist, she 'might have been any one of the many Annes who, during the first half of the seventeenth century, married into or out of the Collins name' (p. ii). Indeed, a check of the computerised International Genealogical Index reveals that there were hundreds of women named 'Anne Collins' (or some variant thereof) living in England during the first half of the seventeenth century. Meanwhile, Sidney Gottlieb has mentioned that the name 'An' could even have been interpreted initially by some contemporary readers as an abbreviation for 'Anthony' (1996, p. vii). Although comments in the poet's volume itself strongly suggest that she was indeed a woman, Gottlieb speaks for practically all scholars when he remarks that we presently 'know nothing about her apart from what we can glean from her one existing book, *Divine Songs and Meditacions* (1653)' (1996, p. vii). To make matters worse, those comments are (as Boyd Berry has wisely emphasised) often so ambiguous as to make firm interpretation nearly impossible (pp. 261, 263).

A good example of these interpretive difficulties concerns the matter of Collins's religious stance. Gottlieb (1996, p. xvii) notes that she 'has been variously identified as a Calvinist (Bell, Parfitt, and Shepherd, 53; Wilcox, 55), an anti-Calvinist (Norbrook, 881), and (perhaps) a Roman Catholic (Greer, 148)'. Ann Hurley describes her as a Calvinist but not rigidly so (p. 165), but Germaine Greer et al. see her as profoundly anti-Calvinist (p. 148). Helen Wilcox identifies her as a Calvinist who was nonetheless 'critical of the radical wing of the parliamentary movement' (p. 55). Meanwhile, Gottlieb wonders about 'the extent to which Collins is, if not a Quaker herself, then at least deeply conversant in and attracted to much of what we associate with mid-seventeenth-century Quakers' (Gottlieb, 1996, pp. xvii–xviii).

Similar disagreements exist about Collins's social and political views. Gottlieb argues that Elaine Hobby, Stanley Stewart, and Helen Wilcox 'overstate or oversimplify her conservativism' (1996, p. xviii), while Greer et al. argue that Collins's apparently conservative attacks on theological innovation are not much different from those of the radical John Milton (p. 151). Elaine Hobby argues that Collins endorses 'reactionary' political positions and that she stresses the need for ecclesiastical and social order and authority (p. 60), but Gottlieb emphasises her sympathy with the need for progressive reformation (1996, p. xviii) and elsewhere argues that her satirical views do not necessarily imply Royalist politics (1997, p. 224). Once again Berry's point seems worth noting: Collins's language in the poems makes it extremely difficult to pin her down precisely on many major issues.

Finally, even the precise nature and causes of Collins's oft-mentioned afflictions are in dispute. Gottlieb concludes, for instance, that 'she may have been sickly, even home-bound or bed-ridden. Physical affliction is a common trope for devotional writers, a predictable metaphor that helps describe the journey from this world to the next. But one senses that illness, weakness, and bodily pain were more than devotional or expressive devices for Collins …' (1996, p. viii). Hurley agrees that 'the stimulus for [Collins's] writing was an acute physical illness that she probably suffered throughout her life' (p. 165). Berry, on the other hand, cautions that the source of Collins's suffering may have been psychological rather than physical: 'nothing in her language would rule out simple, severe depression' (p. 260). Stewart, however, suggests that Collins seems to have been, 'from early childhood, the chronic victim of disease' (p. ii), and Collins's own phrasing – especially her claim that 'Even in my Cradle did my Crosses breed' (p. 4) – strongly supports this claim. There is no reason, after all, that Collins's afflictions could not have been both physical *and* psychological, and she in fact makes clear that they were. Her physical suffering probably helped cause or at least exacerbate her mental depression and spiritual distress. Thus she describes how her 'minde itself, would much torment, / Vpon the rack on restless discontent' (p. 4).

Collins also mentions, however, various other causes of psycho-logical pain – causes that might be justly classified as 'social'. These include her early frustration with others' 'profanenesse' and 'Obscenities' as well as with later instances of 'disgrace or dismall accident, / Indignity or loss' (pp. 6–7). She was sure that 'The wicked ordinarily / Gods dearest children hate', that Satan was perfectly capable of causing his 'agents' to 'vex, oppose, and fret, / To slander and calumniate, / Those that have scap't his net', and that the world was full of fair-weather friends (pp. 37–38). She also expresses sympathy with an unspecified Civil War-era '*Cause* that's now derided so' (p. 66), and she shows her frustration with opponents of order and reformation and with such opponents' tyrranical zealotry (pp. 68–69). Thus the causes of her torment often seem to have been as much the actions and attitudes of other people as the afflictions of her body or soul. She seems to have had, however, a strong conviction of her own inevitable human sinfulness (see, for example, p. 20), and all these torments – physical, mental, spiritual, and social – seem to have influenced not only her life but also the topics and tenor of her poems.

Divine Songs and Meditacions (1653)

Collins's *Divine Songs and Meditacions* is an important text because it is one of the earliest volumes of collected poems by an English woman in the seventeenth-century. The poems are especially intriguing because of the glimpses they provide into the life and mind of a woman writer during this period and because of the social, political, historical, and religious contexts in which they are embedded. Collins's works are also interesting because of their highly varied forms and sometimes striking language. Unfortunately, the poems have rarely been discussed in detail as successful (or unsuccessful) works of art, although one hopes that Collins will increasingly receive such attention from scholars. Commentators have shown much less interest so far in the skill of her writing than in its biographical, religious, or political implications.

As is true of the works of many early modern women writers, critical commentary on Collins's poems has tended to concentrate on topical, thematic, or biographical issues rather than on detailed matters of artistic skill. Thus Gottlieb (1996) emphasises Collins's use of her writing to make sense of her personal pain (p. ix), to engage boldly with public issues (p. x), to defend steadfastly her right to publish (p. x), to engage in political and religious satire (Gottlieb, 1997, pp. 224–25), and specifically to attack the doctrine of mortalism, which asserted that the soul expired when the body died (Gottlieb, 1996, p. xii; see also Gottlieb, 1997, p. 222). Meanwhile, Elaine Hobby stresses the topical and thematic constraints Collins faced when she wrote but also argues that the poet's confinement to mostly traditional religious topics paradoxically gave her greater social authority than if she had spoken in a more consistently personal voice (pp. 59–60). Hobby stresses Collins's social and political conservatism, especially her emphasis on the need for order and contentment (pp. 59–60), but she also argues that Collins uses her work to justify not only feminine celibacy but also women's writing (p. 62). Hurley focuses on Collins's supposedly traditional Protestantism and moderate Calvinism (p. 165; see also Cunnar, p. 49), while Greer et al. suggest that Collins's meditative method may have been influenced by the tradition inaugurated by the Catholic writer Francis de Sales (pp. 150–51). On the other hand, Stewart links her work to the tradition of Puritan diary-writing (p. ii; see also Cunnar, p. 51), while Hurley also emphasises the immediately personal nature of many of the poems: she values Collins for providing insights into the 'spiritual experiences of seventeenth-century women' (p. 165). Stewart underscores Collins's continual thematic focus on God as a regenerating force and source of true peace (p. ii), while Gottlieb argues for her occasionally almost-prophetic boldness (1997, p. 223). Berry, however, sees her as adopting a more frequently apologetic tone (p. 263).

Commentary on Collins's artistry almost always stresses her metrical and stanzaic inventiveness (Hobby, p. 59; Cunnar, p. 51; Hurley, p. 165; Bose, p. 513). Bose notes her interest in 'opportunities for taut argumentation and emphatic self-presentation' and intriguingly argues that her 'preferred idiom fuses the hymn and the lyric' (p. 513). Hurley contends that Collins, 'by avoiding the more conventional disguises of persona or invented characters', often achieves an effect of directness and immediacy, and Hurley also cites the 'detail and range of emotion' of the poems as well as the 'clarity and unmediated directness of her verse', along with its 'modulations of tone from reflection to exaltation and back again' (p. 165). Stewart makes only modest claims for Collins's stature as a poet, emphasising that she was more interested in speaking truth than in displaying skill (p. ii). Gottlieb, meanwhile, offers a typically sane and balanced assessment, arguing that the poems 'are often stylistically and structurally interesting' and contending that although 'some are prosaic and dully catechistical, ... others are lyrical and dramatic' (1996, p. xiii). Gottlieb is presently preparing a detailed commentary on Collins's works, and one hopes that this venture will include close readings of the poems *as* poems.

It may be helpful to highlight some of the more interesting passages from the facsimile pages that follow. Thus Collins claims that because her physical weakness inhibited any 'bodily employments', she was forced into 'a retired Course of life', but she asserts that God granted her a compensating 'inlargednesse of mind, and activity of spirit' that led her to begin composing poetry (sig. [A2r]). Her growing familiarity with Christian truth helped her achieve a 'peaceful temper, and spirituall calmnesse', and she therefore offers her poems primarily to other Christians 'who are of disconsolat Spirits' (sig. [A2v]). Although she anticipates criticism of these products of her '*morning exercise*' (sig. A3r; see also sig. [B1r], p. 2, pp. 63–64), she seems determined both to write and to publish, not only in order to restate standard Christian doctrine but also in order to attack '*Novelties / Whose ground is but the Scum of frothy braines / Perhaps extracted from old Heresies*' (sig. [A4r]). She is modest about the success of her poems *as* poems, but she thinks they have some value if they express truth (sig. [A4v]), and she vows that she will not be hindered 'From publishing those Truths I do intend' (sig. [A4v]; see also p. 63). Although she originally composed her poems for 'private use' (p. 2), she says she decided to publish them in order not only to praise God but also to make proper use of the 'one Tallent' she had been 'bequeath'd', if only so that some 'neare Kindred', by reading her works, might thereby be prompted to 'read the Scriptures touched on in this book' (p. 3) and witness the effects of God's grace in her life (p. 4). She describes her early physical and mental torments (pp. 4–5), her sense of spiritual and social isolation (p. 6), her initial interest in secular writings (p. 6), and then her eventual turn to a focus on the scriptures (pp. 6–7).

The vast majority of Collins's theological pronouncements would have been acceptable to most Christians of her day (see, e.g., pp. 9–27), and it is in such conventional passages that her poems can seem least interesting, especially since her language itself often seems uninventive. Occasionally, however, she expresses more outspoken opinions that give us sudden flashes of individuality, as when she condemns violations of the sabbath caused by 'carnall recreations' (p. 17), or when she attacks 'inferiors [who] disobedient are, / Vngratefull, stubborn, saucy, impudent, / Fayling in reverence, love, respective care, / To their superiors, hating Government' (p. 17), or when she censures such vices as 'lewd pastimes, light gesture, wanton lookes, / Wearing apparell contrary to Sex, / Ill company, vain talk, lascivious books, / And all that may entice like baites or hooks' (p. 18). Similarly interesting are her attacks on vain intellectuals (p. 41), or on those who, during the civil war, sought to compel allegiance and confiscate property from their opponents (p. 64), or on the mortalists, who (she felt) corrupted scripture with their false teachings (pp. 95–96). Her overtly political poems are among the most interesting she composed, partly because they seem most specific in their language and most forceful in the emotions they express (see, e.g., pp. 63–69). She endorses ecclesiastical reform (p. 67), attacks those who resist the reformers (and thereby 'would all Order overthrow' [pp. 67–68]), indicts those who falsely stirred the common people to oppose reform (p. 68), and condemns iconoclasts and violent enemies of peace (pp. 68–69). She herself champions 'the Light of Truth professed / Without obscuring shaddowes old, / When spirits free, not tyed shall be, / To frozen Forms long since compos'd, / When lesser knowledg was disclosed' (p. 69). She feels compelled to speak the truth, not only as a survivor of physical and psychological affliction but also as a survivor of tempestuous times (p. 69).

Not all of Collins's poems are so overtly political, and her five 'Meditacions', in particular, seem less tightly tied to the specific passions of the day. The 'First Meditacion' (pp. 70–74) would seem an effective poem no matter who wrote it; it combines a clear argument with lucid diction, vigorous rhythms, and an engaging humility. Other poems likewise show flashes (or sometimes more than flashes) of impressive skill, as when Collins compares the true believer to 'a Child new born without defect' (p. 25), or when she asserts that a tattered rose is better than a perfect weed (pp. 61–62), or when she condemns the ignorance of 'earthly muckworms' (p. 76). Her poems are full of what would once have been called (in a less skeptical age) enduring wisdom, as when she claims that even if all physical afflictions suddenly disappeared, human beings would still be beset by psychological and spiritual woes (p. 43). The same kind of wisdom is evident when she asserts that melancholy is usually self-defeating, or when she notes that those who complain of their pains often simply add to their afflictions (pp. 50–52).

As a poet, then, Collins offers many potential rewards for modern readers. Her works are interesting not only biographically and historically but also, often, poetically, and the new attention she is now receiving will, one hopes, result not only in a better grasp of her thought but in a richer, fuller appreciation of her rhetorical power and skill.

The *Divine Songs and Meditacions* were first printed in a small octavo volume in London in 1653 by R. Bishop. According to Wing, only one copy of this edition (presently housed at The Huntington Library) now survives. At least two nineteenth-century reference works allude to a later printing (allegedly issued in 1658), but no copy of such an edition is presently known, and indeed such an edition may never have existed (see Stewart, p. i and Gottlieb, 1996, p. xiii). Hurley (p. 165) suggests that the print run of the 1653 edition may have been small. Ownership of the single surviving copy has been traced in detail (see Stewart, p. i and Gottlieb, 1996, xiv). The book was relatively highly priced in the nineteenth and twentieth centuries because of its rarity, but its contents received little sustained attention or appreciation. Stewart (pp. i–ii) quickly reviews the small body of nineteenth-century commentary on the text, while Gottlieb (1996, pp. 123–26) provides a useful bibliography of the relatively few studies added since then. Excerpts from Collins's poems were printed in various collections during the nineteenth century (see Stewart, p. i), and Stewart made a valuable contribution by issuing a facsimile edition (unfortunately abridged) in 1961. The best scholarly edition to date – with a helpful introduction, brief textual notes, and very full commentary – was issued in 1996 by Sidney Gottlieb. Gottlieb makes very few emendations (see Bose, p. 513), although a few of his readings of specific words have been questioned (Berry, pp. 263–64).

The fact that only a single copy of Collins's *Poems and Meditacions* survives makes choosing a base copy a moot issue. Unless and until a better copy than the Huntington Library text appears, we have no other option than to reproduce it. Sidney Gottlieb has succinctly described the salient features of this text: 'The volume is a small octavo, with a page size (cropped) of 136 x 83 mm at the largest dimension, bound in early nineteenth-century English polished calf. It is made up of 52 leaves, gathered as follows: A, 4 leaves; B–G, each eight leaves. ... There is a signature in a mid-seventeenth-century hand at the top of the page headed "To the Reader", but while the first name "William" is clear, what follows is only partially decipherable ...' (Gottlieb, 1996, pp. xiii–xiv). Stewart (p. iii) notes that 'pages have been cropped and the margins have worn away; thus, in some instances (pp. 50, 56, 68), text has been lost'. To make matters even worse, the binding is often very tight, as Gottlieb reports (1996, p. xv). In addition, the text itself is often difficult to read and reproduce because of faintness or other defects. Difficult-to-read passages are therefore transcribed below in an appendix for the convenience of the reader.

References

Wing C5355

Bell, Maureen, George Parfitt, and Simon Shepherd (1990), *A Biographical Dictionary of English Women Writers 1580–1720*, Boston: G.K. Hall

Berry, Boyd M. (1999), Review of Gottlieb (1996), *Journal of English and Germanic Philology*, 98 (2), April

Bose, Mishtooni (1998), Review of Gottlieb (1996), *Review of English Studies*, N.S. 49 (196), November

Cunnar, Eugene R. (1993), 'An Collins' in Hester, M. Thomas (ed.),

Seventeenth-Century British Nondramatic Poets: Third Series, Dictionary of Literary Biography, vol. 131, Detroit: Gale

Gottlieb, Sidney (ed.), (1996), *An Collins: Divine Songs and Meditacions*, Tempe, AZ: Medieval and Renaissance Texts and Studies

Gottlieb, Sidney (1997), 'An Collins and the Experience of Defeat' in Summers, Claude J. and Ted-Larry Pebworth (eds.), *Representing Women in Renaissance England*, Columbia: University of Missouri Press

Greer, Germaine, and Susan Hastings, Jeslyn Medoff, and Melinda Sansone (eds.), (1989), *Kissing the Rod: An Anthology of Seventeenth-Century Women's Verse*, New York: Farrar Straus Giroux

Hobby, Elaine (1989), *Virtue of Necessity: English Women's Writing 1649–88*, Ann Arbor: University of Michigan Press

Hurley, Ann (1998), 'Ann Collins' in Schlueter, Paul and June Schlueter (eds.), *An Encyclopedia of British Women Writers*, New Brunswick, NJ: Rutgers University Press

Norbrook, David (1992), *The Penguin Book of Renaissance Verse 1509–1659*, New York: Penguin

Stevenson, Jane and Peter Davidson (eds.) (2001), *Early Modern Women Poets (1520–1700): An Anthology*, Oxford: Oxford University Press

Stewart, Stanley N. (ed.), (1961), *An Collins: Divine Songs and Meditacions* (1653), Los Angeles: William Andrews Clark Memorial Library

Wilcox, Helen (1989), 'An Collins' in Graham, Elspeth, Hilary Hinds, Elaine Hobby, and Helen Wilcox (eds.), *Her Own Life: Autobiographical Writings by Seventeenth-Century Englishwomen*. New York: Routledge

ROBERT C. EVANS

Acknowledgements

Many thanks to the reference and photographic staffs of The Huntington Library, and also to Sidney Gottlieb. Travel to The Huntington was supported by a research grant from Auburn University Montgomery. For their patience, guidance, and 'close readings', sincere thanks are also due to Patrick Cullen, Anne Lake Prescott, and Betty Travitsky.

Divine Songs and Meditacions (Wing C5355) is reproduced, by permission, from the copy in The Henry E. Huntington Library (shelfmark RB 54047). The book is an octavo with a text block size of 78 × 130 mm.

Difficult-to-read passages are transcribed below in an appendix for the convenience of the reader.

Divine   *Park*

SONGS

and

MEDITACIONS

Compoſed
By
An Collins.

LONDON,
Printed by *R. Biſhop.* Anno Dom. 1653

To the Reader

Christian Reader,

I inform you, that by divine Providence, I have been restrained from bodily employments, suting with my disposicion, which enforced me to a retired Course of life; Wherin it pleased God to give me such inlargednesse of mind, and activity of spirit, so that this seeming desolate condicion, proved to me most delightfull : To be breif, I became affected to Poetry, insomuch that I proceeded to practise the same ; and though the helps I had therein were small, yet the thing it self appeared unto me so amiable, as that it enflamed my faculties, to put forth themselvs, in a practise so pleasing.

Now the furtherances I had herein, was what I could gather (by the benifit of hearing,) at first from prophane Histories; which gave not that satisfactory contentment, before mencioned; but it was the manifest scion of Divine Truth, or rather the Truth it self, that reduced my mind to a peacefull temper, and spirituall calmnesse, taking up my thoughts for Theologicall employments.

Witnesse here of, this Discourse, Songs and Meditacions, following; which I have set forth (as I trust) for the ben.fit, and comfort of others, Cheifly for those Christians who are of disconsolat Spirits, who may perceive herein, the Faithfull-nesse, Love, & Tender Compassionatnesse of God to his people, in that according to his gracious Promise, *He doth not leave nor forsake them.* Heb. **13.5.** But causeth *all things to work for theyr good.* Rom. 8.28. This I doubt not, but most Saints in som measure, do experimentally know, there-fore I will not seek by argument, to prove a thing so perspicuous. And now (Cour-teous Reader) I have delivered unto you, what I intended, onely it remaines that I tell you, That with my Labours, you have my Prayers to God through Jesus Christ; whose I am, and in him,

Yours,
in all Christian affection

An Collins.

The Preface.

BEing through weaknesse to the house confin'd,
My mentall powers seeming long to sleep,
were summond up, by want of wakeing mind
Their wonted course of exercise to keep,
And n.t to waste themselves in slumber deep;
Though no work can bee so from error kept
But some ag. inst it boldly w.ll except:

Yet sith it was my morning exercise
The fruit of intellectuals to vent,
In Songs or counterfets of Poesies,
And haveing therein found no small content,
To keep that course my thoughts are therfore bent,
And rather former workes to vindicate
Than any new concepcion to relate.

Our glorious God his creatures weaknesse sees,
And therefore deales with them accordingly,
Giveing the meanes of knowledg by degrees,
Vnfoulding more and more the Mystery,
And opening the Seales successively,   Rev.6.
So of his goodnesse gives forth demonstracions,
To his Elect in divers Dispensacions.

In legall wise hee did himself expresse
To be the only Lord Omnipotent
A just avenger of all wickednesse,
A jelous God in power eminent,
Which terror workes, and pale astonishment:
Sith plagues for sin are holden forth thereby,
But with no strength to crush inniquity.

Now with the Law the Gospell oft appeares,
But under vailes, perspicuous unto few
Who were as those which of good tydings heares,
Rejoyceing much at the report or show
Of that the Sainte now by possessing knew;
Oft spake the Prophets Evangelicall,
Whose words like kindly drops of rain did fall.

But when the plenerie of time was come
The springs of grace their plesant streams out deald
Felicitie did evidence on her same
Salvacion and the way thereto reveald,
Who wounded were in spirit, might be heald;
Here God declares the Beauties of his Face,
Great Love, rich Mercy, free Eternall Grace,

This time was when the Sonne of Righteousnesse
His Luster in the world began to spread,
Which more and more to his he doth expresse
In termes so large that they that run may read,
And to himselfe he doth the weaker lead;
Into his bosum will his Lambs collect,
And gently those that feeble are direct. Isa. 40. 11

And so in them a life of grace instill
Where'y they shall be able to obay
All Gospell precepts swe'ing with his will,
And that without regard of s·r·all pay,
But with free hearts, where Christ alone doth sway
Causin? the apprehensions of h·s love,
To gender love, which still doth active prove.

Where Christ thus ruleth, I suppose remaines
No heart that hankers after Nov·l·ies
Whose ground is but the Scum of frothy braines
Perhaps extracted from old Heresies,
New form'd with Glosses to deceive the eyes
Of those who like to Children, do incline
To every new device that seemes to shine.

I am perswaded they that relish right,
The Dainties of Religion, Food d·vine,
Have therby such a permanent delight,
And of best Treasures, such a lasting mine,
As that their hearts to change do not i·cline,
I therfore think theyr tastes of Truth is ill,
Who Truths profession quick·y alter will.

I speak not this to manifest desp·ght
To tru Religions growth or augmentacion,
Nor do I take offense of greater L·ght
Which brings probatum eit or commendacion
From Truth it selfe, having tnerto relacion,
But rather with the Saints I doe reic·ence,
When God appeares in his in Gospel·voyes.

                                                    New

Now touching that I hasten to expresse
Concerning these, the offspring of my mind,
Who though they here appeare in homly dresse
And as they are my works, I do not find
But ranked with others, they may go behind,
Yet for theyr matter, I suppose they bee
Not worthlesse quite, whilst they with Truth agree.

Indeed I grant that sounder judgments may
(Directed by a greater Light) declare
The ground of Truth more in a Gospel-way,
But who time past with present will compare
Shall find more mysteries unfolded are,
So that they may who have right information
More plainly shew the path-way to Salvacion.

Yet this cannot prevayl to hinder me
From publishing those Truths I do intend,
As strong perfumes will not concealed be,
And who esteemes the favours of a Freind,
So little, as in silence let them end,
Nor will I therfore only keep in thought,
But tell what God still for my Soule hath wrought.

When Clouds of Melancholy over-cast
My heart, sustaining heavinesse therby,
But long that sad condicion would not last
For soon the Spring of Light would blessedly
Send forth a beam, for helps discovery,
Then dark discomforts would give place to joy,
Which not the World could give or quite destroy.

So

.So sorrow 'erv'd but as springing raine
.To ripen fruits, indowmen's of the mind,
VVho thereby did abillitie attaine
To send forth flowers, of so rare a kinde,
VVhich wither not by force of sun or VVinde:
Retaining vertue in their operations,
VVhich are the matter of those Meditacious.

From whence if evill matter be extracted
Tis only by a wider generacion,
Whose natures are of vennom so compacted,
As that their touch occasions depravacion
Though lighting in the fragramest plantacion:
Let such conceale the evill hence they pluck
And not disgorg themselves of what they sucke

So shall they not the humble sort offend
Who like the Bee, by natures secret act
Convert to sweetnesse, fit for some good end
That which they from small things of worth extract,
Wisely supplying every place that lacke,
By helping to discover what was meant
Where they perceive there is a good intent.

So trusting that the only Sov'rain Power
Which in this work alwaies assisted mee,
Will still remain its firme defensive Tower,
From spite of enemies the same to free
And make it usefull in some sort to bee,
That Rock I trust on whom I doe depend,
Will his and all their works for him defend.

The Discourse.

YOu that indeared are to pietie,
And of a gracious disposicion are,
Delighting greatly in sinceritie
As your respects to godly ones declare;
For whose society you only care:
Dain to survay her works that worthlesse seem,
To such as honnest meanings dis-esteem.

But those that in my love I have preferd
Before all creaturs in this world beside,
Me works, I hope, will never dis-regard,
Though some defects herein may be espide;
Which those that have their judgments rectifide:
Can but discern, yet not with scornfull eye,
As their mild censures cheefly testifie.

Vnto the publick view of every one
I did not purpose these my lines to send,
Which for my private use were made alone:
Or as I said, it any pious friend
Will once vouchsafe to read them to the end:
Let such conceive if error here they find,
Twas want of Art, not true intent of mind.

                                                    Some

Some may desirous bee to understand
What moved mee, who unskilful am herein,
To meddle with, and this to take in hand,
That which I cannot well, end or begin;
But such may first resolve themselves herein,
If they consider, tis not want of skill,
Thats more blame worthy, than want of good will

1   Then know, I cheefly aim that this should bee
Vnto the praise of Gods most blessed name,
For by the mouths of sucking babes doth he,
Reveal his power, and immortall fame;   *Psal.* 8.
Permitting Children to exall the same:
When those that were profound, and worldly wise
In ignominious sort did him despise.

2 Next in respect of that I have receiv'd
Is nothing to that some have, I do confesse,
Yet he to whom one Tallent was bequeath'd,
Was cald to strict account, neverthelesse;
As well as he that many did possess,   *Mat.* 25.
From which I gather, they have no excuse,
Which of ability will make no use.

3 Moreover this is thirdly in respect
Of some neare Kindred, who survive mee may,
The which perhaps do better works neglect,
Yet this, they may be pleased to survay
Through willingnesse to heare what I could say,
VVhereby they may bee haply drawn to look,
And read the Scriptures touched in this book.

4   And lastly in regard of any one,
VVho may by accident hereafter find,
This, though to them the Auther bee unknown,
Yet seeing here, the image of her mind ;
They may conjecture how she was inclin'd :
And further note, that God doth Grace bestow,
Vpon his servants, though hee keeps them low.

Even in my Cradle did my Crosses breed,
And so grew up with me, unto this day,
Whereof variety of Cares proceed,
Which of my selfe, I never could alay,
Nor yet their multip'ying brood destray,
For one distemper could no sooner dy,
But many others would his roome supply,

Yea like the messengers of *Iob*, they hast,
One comes before another can be gon,
All meanes of delight were soon defast,
Finding no matter for to feed upon,
They quickly were disperced every one,
Wher as my minde it selfe, would much torment,
Vpon the lack of endless discontent.

The summers day, though chearfull in it selfe,
Was wearisom, and tedious, unto me,
As those that ere might lack, content or health,
Torment they may soon'it perswaded be,
For by experience truth hereof they see,
Now if the summers day, cause no delight,
How irksome think you was the winters night.

'Twere to no end, but altogether vain,
My feveral croffes namely to expreſſe,
To rub the ſcar would but encreaſe the pain,
And words of pitty would no griefe releaſe,
But rather aggrevate my heavineſs,
Who ever choſe my croffes to conſeale
Till to my griefe they would themſelves reveale

So (to be briefe) I ſpent my infantcy,
And part of freſheſt yeares, as hath been ſayd
Partaking then of nothing cheerfully
Being through frailty apt to be affraid,
And likely ſtill diſtempered or diſmaid,
Through preſent ſeſe of ſome calamity,
Or preconceit of future miſery.

But as the longeſt winter hath an end
So did this fruitleſſe diſcontent expire,
And God in mercy to me refreſhing ſend,
whereby I learn d his goodneſſe to admire,
And alſo larger bleſſings to deſire;
For thoſe that once, have taſted grace indeed,
Will thirſt for more, and craue it till they ſpeed.

But that I may proceed Methodical,
When firſt the extremitie which roſe my minde,
Began to ſettle and to give with all
No more to be ſoſt and at every wade
It ſuch a perſ y exceſſie and rude,
Which wiſe conſiderate Words did ſay,
The ſenſe of ſuffering thud d og convay.
                    S 3   3 r

But liveing where profaneneſſe did abound,
VVhere little goodneſſe might be ſeen or heard ;
Thoſe conſolacions, eould be but unſound
Haveing to godlineſſe no great regard :
Becauſe that of the means I was debard,
Through ignorance of better exerciſe
I then delighted pleſant hiſtories

Whereof the moſt part were but fain'd I knew
Which not-with-ſtanding I no whit diſpiſed,
Imagining although they were not true,
They were convenient being moralized ;
Such vanities I then too highly priſed :
But when profane diſcourſes pleaſd mee beſt
Obſcenities I allwaies did deteſt·

But all this while, the ſumes of vanities
Did interpoſe betwen my ſoules week ſight,
And heavenly bliſſe , devine felicities;
Yntill that morning ſtarr ſo matchleſſe bright
The Sun of righteouſneſſe reveald his light
Vnto my ſoule, which ſweet refreſhings brings,
Becauſe he coms with healing in his wings.

Mal 4 2

Whoſe bleſſed beames my mind eradiates
And makes it ſenſible of pietie,
And ſo by conſequence communicates
Celeſtiall health to ev'ry faculty :
Expeling palpable obſcurity;
Which made my ſoule uncapable of grace,
Which now ſhe much deſires for to imbrace.

perceiving

Perceiving well th at nothing can afford
Her either finall reft, or full content,
But faveing Graces, and Gods holy word,
Which is a means thofe Graces to augment ;
VVith Praier, and the bleffed Sacrament :
VVhich means with reverence my foul affects
And former pleafing vanities rejects.

Together with unnecefary griefe,
VVhofe ill effects can hardly bee expreft,
For certainly it argues unbeleife
Which hinders many from eternall reft ,
who do not feek in time to be redreft; *Heb*.3. 19
Therefore I would eftablifh inward peace,
How. ever out-ward croffes doe increafe.

If crofs difgrace or difmall accident,
Indignity or lofs, befalleth mee,
Immediatly diftempers to prevent,
I cald to mind how all things orderd bee,
Appointed, and difpofed, as we fee.
By Gods moft gracious providence, which is,
I am perfwaded, for the good of his.

Yet am I not fo firm I muft confefs
But many times difcomforts will intru'd,
VVhich oft prevailes to hinder quietne's,
And by that means, fome forrows are remou'd :
VVhich hope will help mee quickly to exclu'ds
So though diftrefs continue for a night,   *Pfal*.
Yet joy returneth by the morning. light.   30.

VVith confidence these favours will increase
My soule hath recolected a'l her powers,
To praise the auther of this blissfull peace,
VVhich no untimely crosse event devouers;
So permanent are the celestiall Flowers:
Those graces which are ever conversent,
VVhere holynes combinds with true content.

O! what trancendant ravishing delights
\Vhat blis unspeakable they doe po'esse,
VVhose merth to holy praises them excites,
And cheers them to go on, in godlynesse,
The very quintissence of happinesse,
As is attainable, or may be had
In this life present, which were elce but bad.

There is a kind of counterset content,
VVherwith some are deceivd, tis to be feard,
VVho think they need not sorrow, or lament,
Being token wall pleasures so indeard;
VVhose minds are stupid, & their concience ceard
I lce might they see all Earthly delectacion,
To be but vanity, and hearts vexacion.   *Eccl.2.*

To light trirjg, carnall merth we may compare,
For as a flash it! astes and soon is gon,
I etetelling of a Thunder clap of care,
It a ioblastes the hear: it lighteth on;
Makes it to goodnesse, fencelels as a ston:
Dra .npevery part, and ra.nity,
Cfi. . . ud body unto piety.

                                    But

But facred joy i like the Sunnes clear light,
VVhich may with clouds, be fometimes overcaft,
Yet breaks it forth anon, and fhines more bright,
VVhofe lively force continually doth laft ;
And fhews moft Orient, when a ftorm is paft :
So true delight may bee eclips'd we fee,
But quite extinguifht, can it never bee.

So now I will go on with my Difcourfe,
VVhen knowledg, plefant to my foul became,
Unto Gods word, I often had recourfe,
Being informed rightly that the fame ;
VVou'd bee as fuell to enceace the flame
Of holy Zeal, which muft with knowledg dwell,
For without other, neither can do well, *Rom.* 10

Then fought I carefully to underftand,
The grounds of true Religion, which impart
Divine Difcrefhion, which goes far beyand,
All civill policy or humane Art ;
VVhich facred principles I got by heart :
VVhich much enabled me to approch nd,
The eace of that whereto I fhall attend.

Firft touching God, there is one God I know,
who hath his being of himfelf alone, *Rom.* 1. 20.
The fountain whence all ftream of goodneffe flow
But bodies, ficts, or paffions hath he none; *Ia.1* 7
And without Decty there is but one; 1 *Cor.* 8. 4.
Eternal, Infinite, and nere to cee 1 *John* 5.7.
One pure effance with diftinctions Three.

The

The firſt whereof for order, is the Father,
The Glorious Fountain of the Trinity,
Having his being, nor begining neither
Of no one but himſelfe, undoubtedly ;
Begets his Sonne, from all eternity,
And with his Sonne, the Holy-Ghoſt forth ſends
From ever-laſting which for aye extends.

The Sonne, the ſecond Glorious perſon is,
For Power, Subſtance, and Eternity,
Alone as is the Father, who it is,
Of whom he hath his being, too, only ;
Yea the whole being of his Father, by
A Sacred and Eternall Genneracion,
A miſtrey paſt all imaginacion.   *Iſaiah.* 53. 8

In Trinity the Holy-Ghoſt is third,
Proceeding and ſo ſent forth equally, *Iohn.* 15.7.
Both from the father & the ſon, or word, *Iohn.* 1.1
Being of their Power, Subſtance, Magiſty ;
And thus diſtinguiſhed are the Trinity :
By whom were all-things made, that ever were,
And by whoſe Providence preſerved are.

VVhat hath been ſayd of God ſhall now ſuffice,
Of whom I frame no Image in my mind,
But I conceive him by his properties,
Hee is incomprehenſible I find ;
Filling all places, in no place confind ;
I will therefore his wondrous works admire,
Not vainly after ſecret things inquire.
                                        Next

Next unto God, my selfe I sought to know,
A thing not so facile, as some suppose,
But that I may the faster forward goe,
I leave to speak, what may bee said of those,
And haste to that I purpose to disclose:
VVhich being well considered may convert,
To lowest thoughts, the proudest haughty heart.

Touching my selfe and others I conceive,
That all men are by nature dead in sin, *Eph. 2. 1.*
And Sathans slaves; not able to receive,
The things of God, which brings true comfort in:
Good actions still they faile in managing;
But apt they are to every vanity,
As vowed servants to inniquiry.

Doe but observe the carnallist how he
Neglects all callings, fitt to be profest,
Waits all occasions, ill implyd to be,
Consumes his wealth, deprives himself of rest;
To please that darling sinn that likes him best:
Iudg what a hellish bondage he is in,
That's Sathans slave, and servant unto sin;

As all men in the state of nature be,
And have been ever since mans wofull fall,
Who was created first, from bondage free,
Untill by sinne he thrust himself in thrall;
By whose transgression we were stained all,
Not only all men but all parts of man,
Corrupted was: since sin to reign began.

The

The Soul who did her makers Image bear,
Which made her amiable fair and bright,
Right Orient and illustrious to appear,
To his omniscient eye and pure sight,
Who doth the inward Purity delight,
Lost all her beauty, once so excellent,
As soon as unto sinn she did content.

The eye of understanding was so bleared,
That no spirituall thing it could behold,
The will corrupted, and the concience ceared,
And all th'affections were to goodnes cold,
But hot to evill, not to be contrould;
The members of the body then proceeds
As instruments to execute bad deeds.

But see what was the consequence of this,
The curse of God which did the fault ensue,
Thus man by sin deprived was of blis,
The thoughts hereof might cause us to eschew
That bitter root whence all our sorrows grew:
Sicknes of body, and distresse of mind,
With all afflictions layd upon mankind.

Whether in body goods or name it be,
And which is worse, the soule's perplexity,
Which concience is awake, from deadnesse free
When she considers what felicity,
She hath exchang'd for endlesse misery;
Cannot torment her else with bootlesse care,
Foreseeing that her pains eternall are.

If this be so, the vileſt liveing creature
Is in a better caſe then man; for why?
When this life ends with ſuch by courſe of nature,
There with is ended all his miſery ;
But man tormented is eternally;
Twere ſo, but that our God we gracious find,
Who ſent a Saviour to reſtore mankind.

The ſecond perſon of the Trinity,   *Iſh.1.1*
The only Son of God omnipotent,
Who being God from all eternity,
To take our nature freely did aſſent,   *Heb.2.16.*
With all afflictons thereto inſident :
In all things, like to other men was he,
Save that from ſins he ſtill remained free.

So that two whole and perfect natures were,
In the ſame perſon joyned really.
And neither of them both, confounded are,
Nor doth the Humane of it ſelfe rely ;
But it ſubſiſteth in the Deity,
Nor can theſe natures ſeperated be,
Both perfect God, and perfect man was he.

This much touching our Saviours perſon ; Now,
His Offices we ought to know likewiſe,
And what he hath performd for us, and how
He freed us from the foreſaid miſeries,
And how Gods dreadfull wrath he ſatisfies;
His Offices ſhall briefly named be,
A Prieſt, a Prophet, and a King, is he.

A Priest, for that he hath for mans transgression
Full satisfaction made to God the father, *Heb.*
And likewise makes continuall intercession, 7.15.
For those who to his fould he means to gather;
Or to eternall heavenly mancions, rather:
The means wherby Gods wrath he satisfies,
Was his obedience and his sacrifice.

The Law of God he perfectly fulfild,
VVith full obedience and integrity,
As God had pre-ordained, then did he yeild
A painfull ignominious death to dy,
The wrath of God appeased was thereby,
Which in full meafure came upon him then,
Even what was due unto the sins of men.

A Prophet to inftruct his Church he is,
Which doth him honour by fincere profession,
His Spirit qualifies the hearts of his,
And makes them pliable to fuch profession,
His word doth take when grace shall have poffef-
For by the word no good efect is wrought [sion,
But where the heart is by Gods spirit taught.

Our Saviour is a King undoubtedly,
Although he seemes to have no Kingdoms here,
Yet in their hearts he means to Glorify,
A Kingdome he erects of grace, and there
Hee raignes, and by his spirit rule doth beare,
But here appears his matchlefle dignity
Hee King of Glory is Eternally.

For when he by his death had finished
The work of our redemcion, freed from paines,
He took his body that before was dead,
With all that to a perfect man pertaines ;
With which he glorioufly afcends and reignes :
At the right hand of God he doth remain
Vntill to Iudgment he returns again.

Chrifts fufferings are fufficient for to free,
All men from wo and endleffe mifery, 2 *Thef.* 3.2
But all men have not faith, and therfore be,
Vnlikely to have benefit thereby,
For it is Faith with which we muft apply,
The merrits of our bleffed Redeemer
And to our felves each in particuler.

Faith is a Grace which doth the foul refine,
Wrought by the Holy-Ghoft in contrite hearts,
And grounded on Gods Promifes divine,
Things fuperexcellent this fame imparts,
To thofe that have it planted in their hearts :
But ere this faith is wrought, the heart muft be,
Made capable of it, in fome degree.

Firft God doth take the hammer of his Law,
And breaks the heart which he for Grace will fit :
Then the feduced foul is brought in aw,
And doth immediatly it felfe fubmitt,
When fight of finne, and forrowing for it,
Hath wrought humility, a vertu rare
VVhich truly doth the foul for Grace prepare.

The Law of God is most exact and pure
Requireing of us perfect holinesse,   *Pfal.* 19.1.
To which is life eternall promit'd sure,
But cursies unto them that it transgresse,
Whether by fraility or by wilfullnesse ;
Though none but Christ, and *Adam* ere his fall
Could keep this Law, yet it may profit all.

For here we may perceive how much we fail,
VVithall what danger we incur thereby,
Then if we can our own defects bewail,
We may for succur to our Saviour fly,
Whose Righteousnesse will all our wants supply ;
Then here are Rules set down for Gods Elect
Whereby they will their course of life direct.

This Law by Gods most skilfull Hand was wrot,
And placed in two Tables orderly,
Shewing what's to be done, and what is not ;
Withall what good or evill coms thereby,
In Ten Commandements so distinctly,
Wherewith as with a Touch stone try we may,
How we offend our God, or him obay.

1 They sin against the first who think or say,
As doth the fool, there is no God at all,
So they that through profanenesse disobay,
And want of knowledg is a breach not small,
Who loves or fears a creature most of all,
And puts trust therein and seeks there-to
Makes that their God, and so break this they do.

                              2 The

2 The second violated is by those
That Images erect, or them adore,
By such also who in devotion goes
To Saint or Angell, succor to implore.
Who set by superstitious Reliques store,
And worship God after mens fantasies,
And not as he commands, breaks this likewise

3 When those that seem religious prove profane,
Gods name is much dishonoured therby;
Even so likewise their error is the same,
Who use his word, or works, or Titles high,
For evill ends, or else unreverently:
By witchcraft, cursing, swearing, blasphemy,
This violated is undoubtedly.

4 Whoso by preparation doth not fit
Himselfe to keep the Sabbath, breaks the same,
As those that holy exercise omit,
Or come thereto only for fear of blame,
Nor have delight or profit by the same;
So it is broke by carnall recreations,
By worldly works, by speech, or cogitations.

5 When that inferiors disobedient are,
Ungratefull, stubborn, saucy, impudent,
Fayling in reverence, love, respective care,
To their superiors, hating Government,
Such grosly break this Fift Commandement:
As those superiors whose bad Disciplin
Or ill example, makes inferiors sin.

6 This

6. This is transgrest by murther, or debate,
By being mindfull of revenge likewise,
By sinfull anger, envy, malice, hate:
By vexing words, and scornfull mockeries,
Which are occasions of extreamities,
Distresse of mind, heart-griefe, perplexity,
And life hath often prejudice thereby,

7 All thoughts impure this Comand'ment breaks,
So lewd pastimes, light gesture, wanton lockes,
Wearing apparell contrary to Sex,
Ill company, vain talk, lascivious books,
And all that may entice like baites or hooks,
To Fornication or Adultery,
VVhich breakes this Precept most apparently.

8 This is transgrest by any kind of stealing,
By coveting our neighbours goods also,
By fraud oppression, or deceitfull dealing,
By not disposing well of that we ow,
Refusing honest works to undergoe,
By being not content with our estate,
Not helping those we should commiserate.

9 This violated is by false witnesse bearing,
Likewise by any Lie we break the same,
By raiseing false reports, or gladly hearing
Ill of our neighbour, touching his good name,
By not maintaining his deserved fame,
By speaking truth of him maliciously
And not exhorting him in secresie.

10 This

10 This is tranfgreft by lufts, and mocions vain
Though we thereto give no confent at all, *Ro.7.7*
As the rebellion of the flefh, or ftain
And blot, we have by finne Originall,
Corrupfion of our nature we it call;
From which becaufe that no one can be free,
Then all tranfgreffors of the Law muft be.

Who by the morrall Law beholds his fin
And fees withall ther's left him no defence,
To forrow therefore now he doth begin,
His Confcience being toucht with lively fence
Of Gods difpleafure for his great offence,
Difpairing of falvation, in refpect
Of ought that by himfelfe he can effect.

The curfe contain'd in this exquifet Law,
Doth work this forrow fo effectually,
For truly he alone is brought in aw,
Whofe Confcience is inform'd of this hereby;
Who breaks but one commandement only
In all his life, and that in coggitacion,
Is not-with-ftanding fubject to damnacion.

Thus when the heart is fitted and prepard,
The feeds of Faith foth-with are caft therein,
VVhich in their orders briefly are declar'd:
The firft is when one wearied under finne,
To feel the wiaght thereof doth now begin
And thereupon acknowledgeth with fpeed
That of a Saviour much he ftands in need;

The

The second is a vehement defire,
Or ardent longing to participate
Of Chrift, and eke his benifits entire
And nothing elſe can this defire abate,
Con unto a limit, quench or mittigate:
As doth the Hart the water brook defire,
So humble Soul's a Saviour doth require.

The third is flying to the Throne of grace,
Even from the ſentence of the Law ſo ſtrict,
Which doth profane ſecurity defaee,
Becauſe that thereby the Conſcience is prict,
Which doth the humb'e man for good afflict
By ſhewing ſuch the danger of their caſe,
And for a cuer, ſending them to grace.

Now this is done by fervent ſupplications,
By conſtant prayer, moſt prevailing known,
Expreſt with hearty ſtrong ejaeculacions,
For Gods eſpeciall grace in him alone,
In the forgivenefſe of his ſins each one ;
And in his prayer, perſevear will hee
Vntil the thing peticion'd, granted bee.

Then God, as he hath promiſed, will prove
Propicious to the ſinner penitent.
And let him feel th'aſſurance of his Love,
His Favour, Grace, and Mercy Excellent
The which in Chriſt, appears moſt emminent:
A holy Faith this full aſſurance is,
Wrought by Gods Spirit, in the hearts of his.

But there are divers meafures or degrees
Of Saving Faith, the leaſt whereof is this,
When he that hath a humble Spirit ſees
He cannot feel, his Faith ſo little is,
As yet the full aſſurance, inward bliſs,
Of the forgivenesse of his ſinnes ſo free,
Yet pardonable findeth them to bee.

And therefore prayeth they may be pardoned,
And with his heart the ſame of God requires,
Recals himſelf, as formerly miſled,
Giveing no reſt unto his large deſires,
His Soul it faints not, nor his Spirit tires,
Although he be delayd yet ſtill he praies,
On God he waites, and for an anſwer ſtaies.

That ſuch a man hath Faith it doth appeare
For theſe deſires doe plainly teſtifie,
He hath the Spirit of his Saviour dear,
For tis his ſpeciall work or property,
To ſtir up longings after purity :
Now where his Spirit is there Chriſt reſides,
And where Chriſt dwels true Faith though **weak**
                                   ſabides

Of ſaveing Faith the largeſt quantity,
Is when a man comes on in Faith untill,
He finds the full aſſurance happily
Of Gods free mercy, favour, and good will,
To him in Chriſt, which doth his joy fulfill:
Finding he hath obtained free remiſſion,
And that he's ſafe in Gods divine tuiſion.

This

This full assurance of his grace and love,
The Lord vouchsafes his servants true who he,
Doth for their inward sanctity approve,
Whose outward doeings also righteous be,
For such alone the evidence may see,
Of his inheritance, true happinesse,
Which for Christs merits sake they shall possesse.

A Christian in his infancy in grace
Finds not this full assurance usually,
Untill he hath been practis'd for a space
By sound Repentance with Sincerity:
And finds Gods Love to him aboundantly
Then shall his soul this full perswasion see,
Which is the strength of Faith or highest degree.

By Faith in Christ much profit we do gain,
For thereby only are we justifide,
At peace with God free from eternall pain,
And thereby only are we sanctifide,
Where faith is, by those fruits, it may be tride:
True faith being by fruits discovered
A barren faith must deeds be false and dead.

Now to be justifide, is to be freed,
From gilt and punishment of sin likewise,
To be accepted as for just indeed,
With God, whose grace it is that justifies;
And not our works, as vainly some surmise:
But that we may still orderly proceed,
It followeth next how we from sin are freed.

The

The sins of those that God will justifie,
Were by Christs sufferings so abolished,
As that they cannot hurt them finally,
VVere they as Scarlet or the Crimson Red,
They shall be white as Snow and cleared, yea is
Even by Christs Blood, the which free was spred
The faithfull, from deserved punishment.

Now comes to be considered how they may
VVith God, for Perfect-just, accepted be,
VVho of themselves by nature (truth to say)
Are in no part from sinnes corruption free,
How such are tane for just, here may we see,
Christs righteousnesse is theirs, by imputation,
And so esteem'd by gracious acceptacion.

The true beleevers benifits are great,
VVhich they by being justified powre,
For such shall stand before Gods judgment seat,
As worthy of Eternall Happinesse,
Even by the merits of Christs Righteousnesse,
For of themselves, they cannot merit ought,
Who are not able to think one good thought.

Then far from doing any work whereby
They might deserve Salvation on their part,
For God whose only perfect purity,
Will find in our best works no true desart,
But rather matter of our endlesse smart :
For in Christs Blood the Saints wch are most dear
Must wash their Robes before they can be clear.

C 4   Though

Though by good works we do not gain Salvacion
Yet these good Duties that our God requires,
We must perform in this our conversacion,
With all our might, endevours, and desires,
Before this short uncertain time expires,
And at perfection must we allwaies aime,
Though in this life we reach not to the same.

For he that by his Faith is justifide,
It followeth also necessarily,
That such by Faith are likwise Sanctifide,
Corrupcion of our nature is thereby
Disabled so, as that inniquity
No longer rules, being by grace subdude,
Whereby the heart to goodnesse is renude.

Corrupcion of our nature purged is,
By vertue of Christs Precious Blood only
Which when by Saving Faith applyed is,
Serves as a corrasive to mortifie
And kill the power of inniquity,
Whence tis that those who Sanctified bee,
From sins deminion, happily are free.

The other part of true Sanctificacion,
Is life or quickenning to holinesse,
And may therefore be called renovacion,
Like a Restorative it doth redresse,
And him revive, that is dead in trespasse ;
Tis by the power of Christs Resurrection,
That we are rais'd from sinne to such perfection.

Sanctificacion

Sanctificacion muft be then entire,
Not for the prefent, perfect in degree,
Yet in refpect of parts and true defire,
Each part and power Sanctified muft bee,
Although no part from all Corruption's free;
Yet every power muft with goodneffe fute,
Though in this life no part be abfolute,

Like as a Child new born without defect,
A perfect man he may be fayd to bee,
Becaufe his body's perfect, in refpect
Of parts, though not in ftature or degree
Of grouth, untill of perfect age he bee ;
So have the faithfull imperfections fome,
Till to a perfect age in Chrift they come.

The graces of the Spirit will appeare,
And fpring up in his heart thats Sanctifide,
And thefe the fruits of Righteoufneffe will beare
Which in his converfacion are difcride,
Thefe graces hath he that is Sanctifide,
A deteftacion of inniquity,
And love to goodneffe, Zeale and Purity,

Whereof Repentance bleffedly proceeds,
Which is endeavour, purpofe or intent
To leave all fin which caufefull forrows breeds
And not to give allowance or confent
To break Gods Law, or leaft Commandtment:
But ever walk exactly there-unto,
Though to the flesh it feemes too much to doe.

So

So that continuall combates will arise,
Between Gods image, on the soul renewde,
And Sathans image, greatest contraries
Which ever seek each other to exclude,
Though in the end, the worst shall be subdude:
Yet in this life it wil in no wise yeeld;
Against whose force, Faith is the only sheild.

Now when a man hath got the victory,
In such a conflict or extream temptacion
He sees Gods love to him abundantly,
By reason of his speciall conservacion,
Which of his favour is a demonstracion;
Now this increaseth peace of conscience most
Together with joy in the Holy-Ghost.

But if the wicked do so far prevaile,
By Gods permission by some provocacion
To over-come the faithfull being fraile,
And subject to be snar'd with temptacion
When not suspecting such abominacion;
But this their fall is through infirmity
Who shall not be forsaken utterly.

For soon a Godly sorrow will arise
And over-flow the heart of such a one,
Which blessedly the same so mollifies,
That it relents for hav.ing so mist gone
Which godly griefe or sorrow is all one
For haveing so displeased God by sinne,
Who hath to him a loveing Father been.

Yea

Yea he for this abhors himſelfe as vile
Acknowledging his execrable caſe,
Till he be reconſil'd to God, that while
Himſelfe by loweſt thoughts he doth abaſe,
As far unworthy to find any grace;
Yet cries to God in this humiliacion
For the return of wonted conſolacion.

And when he hath attain'd recovery,
The breach without delay he fortifies
With ſtronger reſolucion manfully,
And with a Watch impregnable likewiſe,
Againſt aſſaults of this his enimies,
And all aſſaies of their re-entery
Through which ſo many periſh finally.

This much touching the ground of Truth I hold,
VVhich ſith at firſt they rectified my mind,
I will not caſt them off, as worn and old,
Nor will be ſo alone to them confind
As not admit of things of higher kind;
But will as God ſhall light diſpence to mee,
(By ayd divine) walk up to each degree.

A Song expressing their happinesse who have Communion with Christ.

When scorched with distracting care,
  My minde findes out a shade
Which fruitlesse Trees, false fear, dispair
  And melancoly made,
Where neither bird did sing
  Nor fragrant flowers spring,
Nor any plant of use:
  No sound of happynesse.
Had there at all ingresse,
  Such comforts to produce,
But *Sorrow* there frequents,
  The Nurce of Discontents,
And *Murmering* her Mayd
  Whose harsh unpleasant noise
All mentall fruits destroyes.
  Whereby delight's convayd.

Whereof my judgment being certifide
  My mind from thence did move,
For her concepcion so to provide,
  That it might not abortive prove,
Which fruit to signifie
  It was conceaved by
Most true intelligence
  Of this sweet truth divine

Who

Who formed thee is thine, Esay. 54. 5.
   Whence sprang this inference;
He too, thats Lord of all
   Will thee beloved call,
Though all else prove unkind;
   Then chearfull may I sing
Sith I enjoy the Sp ing,
   Though Sesterns dry I find.

For in our Vnion with the Lord alone,
   Consists our happinesse,
Certainly such who are with Christ at one
   He leaves not comfortlesse,
But come to them he will
   Their Souls with joy to fill,
And them to Fortifie
   Their works to undergo
And beare their Crosse also,
   VVith much alacrity:
VVho his assisting grace
   Do feelingly imbrace,
VVith confidence may say,
   Through Christ that strengthens me
No thing so hard I see   Phil 4. 14
   But what perform I may.

But when the Soul no help can see
   Through sins interposicion,
Then quite forlorn that while is she,
   Bewailling her condicion;
In which deplored case

Now such a Soul hath space,
To think how she delayd
Her Saviour to admit
Who shu'd to her for it,
And to this purpose sayd,
Open to me my Love,
My Sister, and my Dove,   Can.5.
My Locks with dew wet are
Yet she remissive grew,
Till he himselfe with-drew
Before she was aware.

But tasting once how sweet he is,
And smelling his perfumes,
Long can she not his presence misse,
But griefe her straimh consumes:
For when he visits one
He cometh not alone,
But brings abundant grace
True Light, and Holynesse
And Spirit to expresse
Ones wants in every case;
For as he wisedome is,
So is he unto his
VVisedome and Purity,   1Cor.1.30
Which when he seemes to hide,
The soul missing her guide,
Must needs confuled lie.

Then let them know, that would enjoy
The firme fruition,

Of

Of his Sweet presence, he will stay
  With single hearts alone,
Who[ut] their former mate,
  Doe quite exterminate:
With all things that desire
  They that are Chrifts, truly,
The Flesh do Crucifie
  With its affections vile   *Gal.5.*
Then grounds of truth are sought
  New Principles are wrought
Of grace and holineffe,
  Which plantings of the heart
Will spring in every part,
  And so it selfe expreffe.

Then shall the Soul like morning bright
  Vnto her Lord appeare,   *Can.6.10*
And as the Moone when full of Light
  So fayr is she and cleare,
With that inherent grace
  Thas darted from the Face
Of Chrift, that Sunne divine,
  Which hath a purging power
Corruption to devour,
  And Conscience to refine ;
Perfection that begun
  As pure as the Sunne,
The Soul shall be likewise
  With that great Bleffedneffe,
Imputed Righteousfeneffe
  Which freely Juftifies.

They that are thus compleat with Grace
   And know that they are so,
For Glory must set Sayle apace
   Whilst wind doth fitly blow,
Now is the tide of Love,
   Now doth the Angell move;
It that there be defect
   That Soul which sin doth wound,
Here now is healing found,
   If she no time neglect;
To whom shall be reveald
   What erst hath been conceald,
When brought unto that Light,
   Which in the Soul doth shine
When he thats most divine,
   Declares his presence bright.

Then he will his beloved shew
   The reason wherefore she
Is seated in a place so low,
   Not from all troubles free;
And wherefore they do thrive
   That wicked works contrive;
Christ telleth his also
   For who as friends he takes
He of his Councell makes,
   And they shall secrets know :   *Iohn* 15. 15
Such need not pine with cares
   Seeing all things are theirs,
If they are Christs indeed;   *Cor.* 3. 21.
   Therefore let such confesse

They are not comfortlesse,
    Nor left in time of Need.

A Song shewing the Mercies of God to his
    people, by interlacing cordiall Com-
        forts with fatherly Chastisments.

AS in the time of Winter
    The Earth doth fruitlesse and barren lie,
Till the Sun his course doth run
Through Aries, Taurus, Gemini ;
Then he repayres what Cold did decay,
Drawing superfluous moistures away,
And by his luster, together with showers,
The Earth becoms fruitfu, & plesant with flowers
That what in winter seemed dead.
There by the Sun is life discovered.

So though that in the Winter
Of sharp Afflictions, fruits seem to dy,
And for that space, the life of Grace
Remayneth in the Root only ;
Yet when the Son of Righteousnesse clear
Shall make Summer with us, our spirits to chear,
Warming our hearts with the sense of his favour,
Then must our flowers of piety favour,
And then the fruits of righteousnesse
We to the glory of God must expresse.

                    D   And

And as wherewigwas parred,
The Sun ascending our Hemisphear,
Ill fumes devouers, and opes the powers
Which in our bodies are, and there
He drawes out the spirits of moving and sence
As from the center, to the circumterence ;
So that the exterior parts are delighted,
And unto mocion and action excited,
And hence it is that with more delight
We undergo labor by day then by night.

So though a Night of Sorrows
May stay proceedings in piety
Yet shall our light like morning bright
Arise out of obscurity,
Then when the Sun that never declines
Shall open the faculties of our mindes,
Stirring up in them that spirituall mocion
Whereby we make towards God with devocion
When kindled by his influence
Our Sacrifice is as pleasing incense.

Now when we feel Gods favour
And the communion with him we have,
Alone we may admit of joy
As having found what most we crave,
Store must we gather while such gleams do last
Against our tryalls sharp winterly blasts
So dispairacion shall swallow us never,   [ever
Who know where God once loves, there he loves
Though sence of it oft wanting is
Yet still Gods mercies continue with his.

So

So soon as we discover
Our souls benummed in such a case,
We may not stay, without delay
W must approach the Throne of Grace,
First taking words to our selves to declare
How dead to goodnesse by nature we are,
Then seeking by him who for us did merit
To be enliv'd by his quickening Spirit,
Whose flame doth light our spark of Grace,
Whereby we may behold his pleased face.

From whence come beams of comfort,
The chiefest matter of tru Content,
Who tast and see, how sweet they be,
Perceive they are most excellent,
Being a glimce of his presence so bright,
Who dwelleth in unapproachable light:
Whoso hath happily this mercy attayned,
Earnest of blessednesse endlesse hath gayned,
Where happinesse doth not decay
There Spring is eternall, and endlesse is day.

*A Song declaring that a Christian may finde
tru Love only where tru Grace is.*

NO Knot of Friendship long can hold
Save that which Grace hath ty'd,
For other causes prove but cold
VVhen their effects are try'd;

D 2   For

For God who loveth unity
    Doth cause the onely union,
Which makes them of one Family
    Of one mind and communion.

Commocions will be in that place,
    VVhere are such contraries,
As is inniquity and grace,
    The greatest enimies,
Whom sin doth rule shee doth command
    To hold stiff opposicion
Gainst grace and all the faithfull band
    Which are in her tuision.

This is the cause of home debates,
    And much domestick woes,
That one may find his houshold mates
    To be his greatest foes,
That with the Wolfe the Lamb may bide
    As free from molestacion,
As Saints with sinners, who reside
    In the same habitacion.

By reason of the Enmity
    Between the womans Seed
And mans infernall enimy,
    The Serpent and his breed,
The link of consanguinity
    Could hold true freindship never,
Neither hath neare affinity
    United freinds for ever.

                              For

For scoffing *Ishmael* will scorn
  His onely true born brother:
Rebeckahs sonns together born
  Contend with one another,
No bond of nature is so strong
   To cause their hearts to tarry
In unity, who do belong
   To masters so contrary.

The wicked ordinarily
  Gods dearest children hate,
And therfore seek (though groundlesly)
   Their credits to abate,
And though their words and works do show
   No colour of offences
Yet are their hearts most (they trow)
   For all their good pretences.

And those that strongest grace attain,
  Whereby sin is vanqu.shed,
By Sathan and his cursed train
  Are most contraried;
Because by such the Serpent feeles,
  His head to be most bruised,
He turnes and catches at their heeles,
  By whom he is so used.

His agents he doth instigate,
  To vex, oppose, and fret,
To slander and calumniate,
  Those that have scap't his net,

D 2
               Who

Who servants are so diligent,
   That like to *Kain* their father
They whose works are most excellent
   They mischiefe will the rather.

Yet there are of the gracelesse crew
   Who for some private ends
Have sided with prefessors tru
   As trusty pious friends,
But to the times of worldly peace
   Their friendship was confined.
Which when some crosses caus'd to cease
   The thred of league untwined.

Such friends unto the *Swallow* may
   Be fitly likened,
Who all the plesant Summer stay
   But are in Winter fled :
They cannot 'bide their freind to see,
   In any kind of trouble,
So pittyfull (forsooth) they bee
   That have the art to double.

Such will be any thing for one
   Who hath of nothing need,
Their freindship stands in word alone,
   And none at all in deed,
How open mouth'd so e're they are,
   They bee as closely handed,
Who will (they know) their service spare,
   They're his to be commanded.

T

Therfore

Therefore let no true hearted one
   Releife at need expect,
From oppofits to vertue known,
   Who can him not afect:
For his internall ornaments,
   Will ever lovely make him
Though all things pleafing outward fence
   Should utterly forfake him.

In choife of Freinds let fuch therefore
   Prefer the godly wife,
To whom he may impart the ftore
   That in his bofome lies:
And let him not pernicioufly
   Communicate his favours,
To all alike indifferently,
   Which fhewes a mind that wavers.

Gods children to each other fhould
   Moft open hearted bee;
Who by the fame preeepts are rul'd,
   And in one Faith agree,
VVho fhall in true felicity,
   Where nothing fhall offend them
Together dwell eternally,
   To which I do eommend them.

A Song demonstrating
The vanities of Earthly things.

SHall Sadnesse perswade me never to sing
But leave unto Syrens that excellent thing,
No that may not be, for truely I find,
The sanguin complexion to mirth is enclin'd.

Moreover, they may who righteousnesse love,
Be soberly merry, and sorrows remove,
They only have right to rejoyeing allwaies
Whose joy may be mixed with prayer and praise.

Wherefore rejoyceth the epicure?
As though his sadeing delights would endure,
VVhereas they are ended, as soon as begun,
For all things are vanity under the Sun.

Riches and Honour, Fame and Promocion,
Idols, to whom the most do their devocion;
How sadeing they are, I need not to show,
For this by experience, too many doe know.

They that delight in costly attire,
If they can compasse the things they desire,
Have onely obtained, what sin first procured,
And many to folly are therby alured.

                                    Learning

Learning is sure an excellent thing,
From whence all Arts and sciences spring,
Yet is it not from vanity free,
For many great Scholars prophane often be.

Whoso hath studied Geometry,
Or gained experience in Geography,
By tedious labour much knowledg may gain,
Yet in the conclusion, hee'l find all is vain.

He that hath studied Astronomy,
Though his meditacion ascend to the Sky
He may mis of heaven and heavenly blis,
If that he can practise no studdy but this,

But they that delight in Divinity,
And to be exquisit in Theology,
Much heavenly comfort in this life may gain,
And when it is ended their joyes shall remain.

VVhat should I speak more of vanities,
To use many words when few may suffice,
It argueth folly, therfore I have don,
Concluding, all's vanity under the Sun.

A Song manifesting
The Saints eternall Happinesse

SOund is the Minde
    Which doth that Hope possesse
Whose object is Eternall joy
  Or Heavens Happinesse;
Such healthfull hearts
    Their spirits doe sustain,
In thinking on the Rest which for
  God; peeple doth remain,
A Treasure inaccessible,
  Or Everlasting Life,
A blessed State which never shall
  be cumbered with strife   *Heb.4.6*

Salvacion
  With endlesse Glory cleare,   *2 Tim.2.10*
And each good thing to be desir'd
  Are in their Fountain there;
Flowers are here,
  Together with the weeds
Exposed to all kinde of stormes,
  Which much confusion breeds:
Some for weaknesse are dismaid,
  And some are comfortlesse,
Because of some defect of sence,
  Or want of comlinesse.

                       Grant

Grant some may have
   Proporcion so compleat,
That correspondency of parts
   Declares Perfections seat
Yet doub les such
   Their bu. then have also
By reason of their travellwhich
   They needs must undergo,
For in every calling is
   A tedious wearinesse
Which whoso followes carefully
   Is driven to confesse

Further suppose
   One might be freed from all
Afflictions which externall are,
   Or crosses corporall
Yet if the soule
   Be seneible of sin
It cannot be but such will have
   Enough to do within:
For to Preserve the heart and waies
   From being over grown
With fruits of that contagious seed
   That's in our nature sown.

Doubting some times
   The Soul with anguish tires,
Who must anon encounter with
   inordinate desires :

                      Lust

Lust oft prevailes,
　　And then the consequence,
Will be a great ecclips of grace,
　　And losse of comfort sence,
In striving to recover peace,
　　The soule is oft opprest.
As he that's conscious of his sin,
　　Hath here but little rest.

From all those woes
　　And many more that bee,
The Sant that finisht hath his course
　　Shall be for ever free,
And likewise have
　　For ever to posesse
A most exquisit Diadem,
　　The Crown of righteousnesse,　　2. Tim. 4. 8.
Of that divine inheritance
　　Which fadeth not away,　　1. Pet. 1. 5.
They shall be really potest,
　　And ever it enjoy.

Bodies which here
　　Are matter thick and grosse,
Attaining to this happinesse,
　　Are freed from their drosse;
And as the Sunn
　　Appeares in brightest Sky,　　Mat. 13. 43.
So every body glorifi'd
　　Shall be for clarity,

　　　　　　　　　　　And

And likewise be impaffible,
   Uncapable of pain
Having agility to move.
   VVhofe vigour fhall remain.

Glorified Soules,
   Are fild with all delight,
Becaufe the fpring of Beury is
   The object of their fight:
Alfo they have,
   (Their joy to amplify)
Immediat fweet communion with
   The bleffed Trinity.
Which fatisfies the apperite,
   Which elfe were empty ftill,
Becaufe no finite comfort can
   Content the mind and will.

Briefly a word
   O place and company
Which Saints in G o y fhall enioy,
   The place is heaven.y   *Heb.1 3.*
Ierufalem,
   The citty of the Lord:
Difcover'd by fuch precious things   *Rev.2 1.*
   As pleafure moft affo d,
The conforts, Angelis numberleffe,
   The whole Affembly   *Heb.1 2.*
Of Saints, who fhall for ever dwell
   With Chrift Eternally.

                        Why

VVhy hath the Lord
   For his, such Ioyes prepar'd
Because their pacient sufferings
   He richly will reward,
This light distresse   2 Cor. 4. 17
   Which for a moment dures
An excellent eternall waight
   Of Glory his procures,
But our afflictions merit not   Rom. 8. 18.
   This Glory that exceeds
But it. as Gods all other gifts,
   Of his free-Love proceeds.   Rom. 6. 23.

Now they that have
   This Hope of Heaven sure,
Shew it by striving to be cleane
   As Christ our Lord is pure,   1 Iohn: 3. 3.
Also they take
   Their croses chearfully
Because a substance they expect,
   Eternall heavenly,   Heb. 10. 34.
To which my Soule aspired still
   And cannot setled be,
Till shee returns againe to him
   That gave her unto me.   Ecl. 12. 7.

A Song exciting to spirituall Alacrity.

Discomforts will the heart contract
   And joy will cause it to dilate;
That every part its part may act,
   A heart enlarg'd must animate.

Unfruitfull ones therfore they are
   That planted be in sorrow's shade,
Sith by the blasts of cloudy care
   They are unfit for action made.

The ill effects of fruitlesse greife
   Are in this place no further shown,
Because the meanes of true releife
   Is more convenient to be known.

Now he in whom all fullnesse dwels   *Col.1 9:*
   All good and meanes of good must bee,
His presence Sathans rule expells
   And doth from Legall terror free.   *Gal.3.13.*

So that their Soules which are so blessed
   His sacred presence to enioy,
Can never be so much distressed
   But consolacion find they may.

                           Having

Having a hiding place secure,   *Isay.32.1.2*
   And covert from the stormy wind,
And streames of water perfect pure
   To vivify and cheare the mind.

If scorched with afflictions heat
   They to their shady rock may fly,
And be in safties bosome seat
   And lap of true felicity.

Where are delights Angelicall,
   The quintissence of all good things,
Refined wine to cheare withall
   And food which life eternall brings.

Which though the Saints by faith posesse,
   Doe not suppose it solace give,
But truly reall happinesse,
   As they that feele alone beleeve.

Who thence abundant strength collect,
   In all condicions to support,
Nor cubles can them much deject,
   Who have this soules defensive Fort.

Suppose temptacion sift them sore,
   Sufficient grace will them releive, *2 Cor.12.9.*
And make their Faith appeare the more,
   Which will to them the Conquest give.

Or be their Scourge some outward Crosse,
    As causlesse hate, or poverty,
Decay of parts, disease, or losse
    Of Credit, Freinds, or Liberty.

Nay were their state compos'd of woes,
    In whom the Morning Star doth shine,
Whose lively luster will disclose,
    To his a heritage divine,

Which he of Love did them procure,
    With freedom, not to *Adam* dain'd
To tast the Tree of Life most pure,
    Whereby the soule alone 's sustain'd

The sence of Love-Eternall, doth,
    with Love, Obedience still produce,
Which active is, and passive both,
    So suffrings are of speciall use.

Bearing the soule with joy and peace,
    Through true beleeving, evermore,
Whose sweet contentments take encrease;
    From heavens never-fayling store.

Another Song exciting to spirituall Mirth.

THe Winter being over
  In order comes the Spring,
Which doth green Hearbs discover
  and cause the Birds to sing;
The Night also expired,
  then comes the Morning bright,
Which is so much desired
  by all that love the Light ;
  this may learn
  them that mourn
To put their Griefe to flight.
The Spring succeedeth Winter,
  and Day must follow Night.

He therefore that sustaineth
  Affliction or Distresse,
Which ev'ry member paineth,
  and findeth no resesse ;
Let such therefore despaire not,
  but on firm Hope depend
Those Griefes immortall are not,
  and therefore must have end :
  they that faint
  with complaint

Therefore

Therefore are too blame,
They ad to their afflictions,
And amplify the fame.

For if they could with patience
A while poſeſſe the minde,
By inward Conſolacions
They might refreſhing finde,
To ſweeten all their Croſſes
That little time they 'dure;
So might they gain by loſſes,
And ſharp would ſweet procure.
But if the minde
Be inclinde
To Vnquietneſſe
That only may be called
The worſt of all Diſtreſſe.

He that is melancolly
Deteſting all Delight,
His Wits by ſottiſh Folly
Are ruinated quite:
Sad Diſcontent and Murmors
To him are inſident,
Were he poſeſt of Honors,
He could not be content:
Sparks of joy
Fly away,
Floods of Cares ariſe,
And all delightfull Mocions
In the conception dies.

But

But those that are contented
However things doe fall,
Much Anguish is prevented,
And they soon freed from all ;
They finish all their Labours
With much felicity,
Theyr joy in Troubles savours
Of perfect Piety,
Chearfulnesse
Doth expresse
A setled pious minde
Which is not prone to grudging
From murmoring refinde.

Lascivious joy I prayse not,
Neither do it allow,
For where the same decayes not
No branch of peace can grow ;
For why, it is sinister
As is excessive Griefe,
And doth the Heart sequester
From all good : to be briefe,
Vain Delight
Passeth quite
The bounds of modesty,
And makes one apt to nothing
But sensuality.

This song sheweth that God is the strength
of his People, whence they have
support and comfort.

MY straying thoughts, reduced stay,
And so a while retired,
Such observations to survay
VVhich memory hath registred,
That were not in oblivion dead.

In which reveiw of mentall store,
One note affordeth comforts best,
Cheifly to be preferd therfore,
As in a Cabinet or Chest
One jewell may exceed the rest.

God is the Rock of his Elect
In whom his grace is incoate,
This note, my soule did most affect,
It doth such power intimate
To comfort and corroberate.

God is a Rock first in respect
He shadows his from hurtfull heat,
Then in regard he doth protect
His servants still from dangers great
And so their enimies defeat.

E 2   In

In some dry desart Lands (they say)
Are mighty Rocks, which shadow make,
Where passengers that go that way,
May rest, and so refreshing take,
Their sweltish Wearinesse to slake.

So in this world such violent
Occasions, find we still to mourn,
That scorching heat of Discontent
VVould all into combustion turn
And soon our soules with anguish burn,

Did not our Rock preserve us still,
Whose Spirit, ours animates,
That wind that bloweth where it will   *Iohn.*3.8
Sweetly our soules refrigerates,
And so distructive heat abates.

From this our Rock proceeds likewise,
Those living streames, which graciously
Relieves the soule which scorched lies,
Through sence of Gods displeasure high,
Due to her for inniquity.

So this our Rock refreshing yeelds,
To those that unto him adhere,
Whom likewise mightily he sheilds,
So that they need not faint nor fear
Though all the world against them were.

                                   Because

Becaufe he is their ftrength and tower,
Whofe power none can equalize,
VVhich onely gives the ufe of power
Which juftly he to them denies,
Who would againft his fervants rife.

Not by felfe power nor by might,
But by Gods fpirit certainly,   *Zach.*4.
Men compaffe and attain their right,
For what art thou O mountain high!
Thou fhalt with valleys, even ly.

Happy was *ifraell*, and why,
Jehovah was his Rock alone,   *Deu.*33.29
The *Sword of his Excellency*,
His fheild of Glory mighty known,
In faving thofe that are his own.

Experience of all ages fhewes,
That fuch could never be dimayd
Who did by Faith on God repofe,
Confeffing him their onely ayd,
Such were alone in fafty ftayd.

One may have freinds, who have a will
To further his felicity,
And yet be wanting to him ftill,
Becaufe of imbecility,
In power and ability.

          E 4   B

ut whom the Lord is pleas'd to save,
uch he is able to defend,
is grace and might no limmits have,
And therefore can to all extend
Vho doe or shall on him depend.

Nor stands he therefore surely,
Vhose Freinds most powerfull appeare,
Because of mutabillity
To which all mortalls subject are,
Vhose favours run now here, now there.

ut in our Rock and mighty Fort,
Of change no shadow doth remain,
His favours he doth not Transport
s trifles movable and vain,
is Love alone is lasting gain.

herfore my soule do thou depend,
pon that Rock which will not move,
Vhen all created help shall end
hy Rock impregnable will prove,
Vhom still embrace with ardent Love.

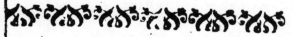

Another Song.

THe Winter of my infancy being over-past
hen supposed, suddenly the Spring would hast
Vhich useth every thing to cheare
ich invitacion to recreacion
is time of yeare,

The

[the ground

The Sun sends forth his radient beames to warm.
The drops distil, between the gleams delights abo-
Ver brings her mate the flowery Queen,   [und,
The Groves shee dresses, her Art expresses
On every Green.

But in my Spring it was not so, but contrary,
For no delightfull flowers grew to please the eye,
No hopefull bud, nor fruitfull bough,
No moderat showers which causeth flowers
To spring and grow.

My Aprill was exceeding dry, therfore unkind;
Whence tis that small utility I look to find,
For when that Aprill is so dry,
(As hath been spoken) it doth betoken
Much scarcity.

Thus is my Spring now almost past in heavinesse
The Sky of pleasure 's over-cast with sad distresse
For by a comfortlesse Eclips,
Disconsolacion and sore vexacion,
My blossom nips.

Yet as a garden is my mind enclosed fast
Being to safety so confind from storm and blast
Apt to produce a fruit most rare,
That is not common with every woman
That fruitfull are.

A Love of goodnesse is the cheifest plant therin
The second is, (for to be briefe) Dislike to sin.

These grow in spight of misery,
VVhich Grace doth nourish and cause to flourish
Continually.

But evill motions, currupt seeds, fall here also
whence springs prophanesse as do weeds where flowers grow
VVhich must supplanted be with speed
These weeds of Error, Distrust and Terror,
Lest woe succeed

So shall they not molest, the plants before exprest
Which countervails these outward wants, & purchase rest
Which more commodious is for me
Then outward pleasures or earthly treasures
Enjoyd would be.

My little Hopes of worldly Gain I fret not at,
As yet I do this Hope retain; though Spring be lat
Perhaps my Sommer-age may be,
Not prejudiciall, but benificiall
In ough for me.

Admit the worst it be not so, but stormy too,
Ile learn my selfe to undergo more then I doe
And still content my selfe with this
Sweet Meditacion and Contemplacion
O heavenly blis,

VVhich for the Saints reserved is who persevere
in Piety and Holynesse, and godly Feare,
The pleasures of which blis divine
Neither Logician nor Rhetorician
Can well define.

Finis.

Another Song.

HAving restrained Discontent,
  The onely Foe to Health and Witt,
I sought by all meanes to prevent
The causes wh ch did nourish it.
Knowing that they who are judicious
Have alwaies held it most pern cious.

Looking to outward things, I found
Not that which Sorrow might abate,
But rather cause them to abound
Then any Greife to mittigate
Which made me seek by supplicacion
Internall Peace and Consolacion

Calling to mind their wretchednesse
That seem to be in happy case
Having externall happinesse
But therewithall no inward grace;
Nor are their minds with knowledge poss she
In such all vertues are al o......c

For where the mind 's obscure and dark
There is no vertu resident,
Of goodnesse there remaines no spark
Distrustfullnesse doth there freque..:
For Ignorance the cause of error
May also be the cause of terror

As doth the Sun-beames beautify
The Sky, which else doth dim appeare
So Knowledg doth exquisitly
The Mind adorn, delight and cleare
Which otherwise is most obscure,
Full of enormities impure.

So that their Soules polluted are
That live in blockish Ignorance,
Which doth their miseries declare
And argues plainly that their wants
More hurtfull are then outward Crosses
Infirmities, Reproach, or Losses.

Where saving Knowledg doth abide,
The peace of Conscience also dwels
And many Vertues more beside
Which all obsurdities expels,
And fils the Soule with joy Celestiall
That shee regards not things Terrestiall.

Sith then the Graces of the Mind
Exceeds all outward Happinesse,
What sweet Contentment do they find
Who are admitted to possesse
Such matchlesse Pearles, so may we call them,
For Precious is the least of all them.

VVhich when I well considered
My greife for outward crosses ceast,
Being not much discouraged

Although

Although afflictions ſtill encreaſt,
Knowing right well that Tribulacion
No token is of Reprobaciun.

Another Song.

EXceſſive worldy Greife the Soule devouers
And ſpoyles the activneſſe of all the Powers,
Through indiſpoſing them to exerciſe
What ſhould demonſtrate their abilities,
By practicall improvment of the ſame,
Unto the Glory of the givers name.
Though Envy wait to blaſt the Bloſſoms green
O' any Vertu ſoon as they are ſeen,
Yet none may therfore juſtice aſhon take
To ſhun what Vertu manifeſt ſhould make,
For Like the Sun ſhall Vertu be beheld
VVhen Clouds of Envy ſhal be quite diſpeld;
Though there be ſome of no diſtaſt at all
Who no degree in worth can lower fall,
Preter'd before the Vertuous whom they taunt
Onely becauſe of ſome apparent want,
Which is as if a Weed without defect
Before the Damask Roſe ſhould have reſpect,
                                   Becauſe

Becauſe the Roſe a leaſe or two hath loſt,
And this the Weed of all his parts can boaſt;
Or elce as if a monſtrous Clout ſhould be
Prefer'd before the pureſt Lawn to ſee.
Becauſe the Lawn hath ſpots and this the Clout
Is equally polluted thoroughout
Therefore let ſuch whoſe vertu favours merits,
Shew their divinly magnanimious ſpirits
Ev diſregarding ſuch their approbacion
Who have the worthleſſe moſt in eſtimacion,
For who loves God above all things, not one
Who underſtands not that in him alone
All cauſes that may move affection are,
Glimpſes wherof his creatures doe declare,
This being ſo, who can be troubled
When as his gifts are undervalued,
Seeing the giver of all things likewiſe
For want of knowledg many underpriſe.

*A Song composed in time of the Civill
Warr, when the wicked did much
insult over the godly.*

VVIth *Sibells* I cannot Devine
    Of future things to treat,
Nor with *Parnassus* Virgins Nine
    Compose in Poëms neat
Such mentall mocions which are free
    Conceptions of the mind,
Which notwithstanding will not be
    To thoughts alone confind.

With *Deborah* twere joy to sing
    When that the Land hath Rest,
And when that Truth shall freshly spring,
    Which seemeth now deceast,
But some may waiting for the same
    Go on in expectacion
Till quick conceipt be out of frame,
    Or till Lifes expiracion.

Therefore who can, and will not speak
    Betimes in Truths defence,
Seeing her Foes their malice wreak,
    And some with smooth pretence

                     And

And colours which although they glose
  Yet being not ingra ind,
In time they shall their luster lose
  As cloth most foully staind.

See how the Foes of Truth devise
  Her followers to defame,
First by Aspersions false and Lies
  To kill them in good Name;
Yet here they will in no wise cease
  But Sathans coutse they take
To spoyl their Goods and Wealths increase,
  And so at Life they make.

Such with the Devill further go
  The Soule to circumvent
In that they seeds of Error sow
  And to false Worships tempt,
And Scriptures falsly they apply
  Their Errors to maintain,
Opposing Truth implicitly
  The greater side to gain.

And to bind Soul and Body both
  To Sathans service sure
Therto they many ty by Oath,
  Or cause them to endure
The Losse of lightsom Liberty
  And suffer Confiscacion,
A multitude they force therby
  To hazard their Salvacion.

Another

Another fort of Enimies
  To Lady Verity,
Are fuch who no Religion prife,
  But Carnall Liberty.
Is that for which they doe conteſt
  And venture Life and State,
Spurning at all good meanes expreſt,
  The force of Vice to bate.

Yet thefe are they, as fome conceit,
  Who muſt again reduce,
And all things fet in order ſtrait
  Difjoynted by abuſe,
And wakeing witts may think no leſſe
  if Fiends and Furies fell,
May be fuppoſ'd to have fucceſſe
  Diſorders to expell.

How-ever Truth to fade appeare,
  Yet can ſhee never fall,
Her Freinds have no abiding here,
  And may feem waſted all;
Yet ſhall a holy Seed remain
  The Truth to vindicate,
Who will the wrongeds Right regain
  And Order elevate.

VVhat time Promotion, Wealth, and Peace,
  The Owners ſhall enjoy,
Whofe Light ſhall as the Sun encreafe
  Unto the perfeſt Day

Then shall the Earth with blessings flow,
    And Knowledg shall abound,
The *Cause* that's now derided so,
    Shall then most just be found.

Prophanesse must be fully grown,
    And such as it defend
Must be mind or overthrown,
    And to their place defend,
The Sonns of strife their force must cease,
    Having fulfild their crime,
And then the Son of wished peace
    Our Horizon will clime.

That there are such auspicious dayes
    To come, we may not doubt,
Because the Gospels splendant rayes
    Must shine the World throughout:
By Iewes the Faith shall be embrac't
    The Man of Sin must fall,
New Babell shall be quite defac't
    With her devices all.

Then Truth will spread and high appeare,
    As grain when weeds are gon,
Which may the Sain s afflicted cheare
    Oft thinking hereupon;
Sith they have union with that sort
    To whom all good is ty'd
They can in no wise want support
    Though most severely try'd.

Another Song

Time paſt we underſtood by ſtory
   The ſtrength of Sin a Land to waſte,
Now God to manifeſt his Glory.
The truth hereof did let us taſte,
For many years, this Land appears
Of uſefull thinʒs the Nurſery,
Refreſht and fenc'd with unity.

But that which crown'd each other Bleſſing
Was evidence of Truth Divine,
The Word of Grace ſuch Light expreſſing,
Which in ſome prudent Hearts did ſhine,
Whoſe Flame inclines thoſe noble minds
To ſtop the Courſe of Prophanacion
And ſo make way for Reformacion.

But He that watcheth to devour,
  This their intent did ſoon diſcry,
For which he ſtrait improves his powe:
This worthy work to nullify
With Sophiſtry and Tiranny,
His agents he forthwith did fill
Who gladly execute his will.

And firſt they prove by Elocution
And Helliſh Logick to traduce
Thoſe that would put in execucion,
Reſtraint of every known abuſe;

ey seperate and 'sturb the State,
nd would all Order overthrow,
he better sort were charged so.

ch false Reports did fill all places,
orrupting some of each degree,
o whom the highest Title graces
rom hearing slanders was not free,
Which Scruple bred, and put the Head
ith prime't members so at bate
Which did the Body dislocate.

Lying Spirit mis-informed
e common peeple, who suppose
things went on to be reformed
ey should their ancient Customs lose,
nd be beside to courses ty'd
hich they nor yet their Fathers knew,
d so be wrapt in fangles new.

reat multitudes therefore were joyned
o Sathans plyant instruments,
ith mallice, ignorance combined,
d both at Truth their fury vents;
ist Piety as Enimy
ey persecute, oppose, revile,
en Freind as well as Foe they spoyle.

e beuty of the Land's abollisht,
h Fabericks by Art contriv'd,
e many of them quite demollisht,
d many of their homes depriv'd   Some

Some mourn for freinds untimely ends,
And some for necessaries faint,
With which they parted by constraint.

But from those storms hath God preserved
A people to record his praise,
Who sith they were therefore reserved
Must to the heigth their Spirits raise
To magnify his lenity,
Who safely brought them through the fire
To let them see their hearts desire

Which many faithfull ones deceased
With teares desired to behold,
Which is the Light of Truth professed
Without obscuring shaddowes old,
When spirits free, not tyed shall be
To frozen Forms long since compos'd,
When lesser knowledg was disclos'd.

VVho are preserv'd from foes outragious,
Noteing the Lords unfound-out wayes.
Should strive to leave to after-ages
Some memorandums of his praise,
That others may admiring say
Unsearchable his judgments are,
As do his works alwayes declare.

F 3

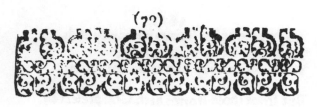

Meditacions

The first Meditacion.

THe Morning is at hand, my Soule awake,
  Rise from the sleep of dull security;
Now is the time, anon 'twill be too late,
Now hast thou golden opportunity
For to behold thy naturall estate
And to repent and be regenerate.

Delay no longer though the Flesh thee tell
Tis time enough hereafter to repent,
Strive earnestly such mocions to expell,
Remember this try courage to augment
The first fruits God requir'd for sacrifice,
The later he esteemed of no price.

First let's behold our natural estate
How dangerous and damnable it is,
And thereupon grow to exceeding hate
With that which is the onely cause of this;
The which is Sin, yea Disobedience
Even that which was our first parents offence.

The reasonable Soule undoubtedly
Created was at first free from offence,
In Wisdom, Holinesse, and Purity,
It did resemble th· Divine Essence,
Which being lost, the Soule of man became
Like to the Serpent, cause of the same.

The Understanding. Will, Affections cleare,
Each part of Soule and Body instantly
Losing their purity, corrupted were
Throughout as by a loathsom Leprocy
The rayes of Vertu were extinguisht quite
And Vice usurpeth rule with force and might.

This sudden change from sanctitude to sin
Could but prognosticat a fearfull end,
Immediatly the dollour did begin,   (send,
The Curse that was pronounc'd none might de-
Which Curse is in this life a part of some,
The fulnesse thereof in the life to come·

The Curse that to the Body common is
The sence of Hunger, Thirst, of Sicknes, Pains
The Soules Callamities exceedeth this,
A Taft of Hell, shee often doth instain,
Rebukes of Conscience, threatning plagues for sin,
A world of Torments oft shee hath within.

F 4   Unlesse

Unlesse the Conscience dead and seared be,
Then runs the soule in errors manifold,
Her danger deep shee can in no wise see,
And therefore unto every sin is bold,
The Conscience sleeps, the Soule is dead in sin,
Nere thinks of Hell untill shee comes therein.

Thus is the Conscience of the Reprobate,
Either accusing unto desperacion,
Or elce benummed, cannot instigate
Nor put the Soule in mind of reformacion;
Both work for ill unto the castaway,   play.
Though here they spent their time in mirth and

Yet can they have no sound contentment here,
In midst of laughter oft the heart is sad:
This world is full of woe & hellish feare
And yeelds forth nothing long to make us glad
As they that in the state of nature dy
Passe but from misery to misery.

Consider this my soule, yet not despaire,
To comfort thee again let this suffice,
There is a Well of grace, whereto repaire,
First wash away thy foul enormities
With teares proceeding from a contrite heart,
With thy beloved sins thou must depart.

                                    Inordinate

Inordinate affections, and thy Will,
And carnall wisdom, must thou mortify,
For why, they are corrupt, prophane and ill,
And prone to nothing but impiety,
Yet shalt thou not their nature quite deface,
Their ruines must renewed be by grace.

If that thou canst unfainedly repent,
With hatred therunto thy sins confesse,
And not because thou fearest punishment
But that therby thou didst Gods Laws transgress
Resolving henceforth to be circumspect,
Desiring God to frame thy wayes direct.

Each member of thy body thou dost guide,
Then exercise them in Gods service most
Let every part be throughly sanctifide
As a meet Temple for the Holy Ghost;
Sin must not in our mortall bodies raign
It must expelled be although with pain

Thou must not willingly one sin detain,
For so thou mayst debarred be of blis,
Grace with inniquity will not remain,
Twixt Christ and Belial no communion is,
Therefore be carefull every sin to fly,
And see thou persevere in piety.

So

So mayſt thou be perſwaded certainly,
The Curſe ſhall in no wiſe endanger thee,
Although the body ſuffer miſery
Yet from the ſecond death thou ſhalt be free;
They that are called here to Holineſſe
Are ſure elected to eternall bliſſe.

A Taſte of bleſſedneſſe here ſhalt thou ſay,
Thy Conſcience ſhall be at Tranquility,
And in the Life to com thou ſhalt enjoy
The ſweet fruict of the Trinity,
Society with Saints then ſhalt thou have,
Which in this life thou didſt ſo often crave.

Let this then ſtir thee up to purity,
Newneſſe of life, and ſpeedy Converſion,
To Holineſſe and to integrity,
Make conſcience of impure thoughts unknown
Pray in the Spirit with ſweet Contemplacion
Be vigilant for to avoid Temptacion.

The Preamble.

Amid the Ocean of Adverſity,
Neare whelmsed in the Waves of ſore Vexation,
Tormented with the Floods of Miſery,
And almoſt in the Gulfe of Deſpairacion,
Neare deſtitute of Comfort, full of Woes,
This was her Caſe that did the ſame compoſe:

At length Jehovah by his power divine,
This great tempeſtious Storm did mittigate.
And cauſe the Sun of Rightcouſneſſe to ſhine
Upon his Child that ſeemed deſolate,
Who was refreſhed, and that immediatly,
And Sings as follows with alacrity.

The ſecond Meditacion.

THe ſtorm of Anguiſh being over-blown,
To praiſe Gods mercies now I may have
For that I was not finally orethrown, (ſpace,
But was ſupported by his ſpeciall grace;
The Firmament his glory doth declare, *Pſal.*19.1
Yet over all his works, his mercies are.*Pſal,*145.9

The Contempʼacion of his mercies ſweet,
Hath raviſhed my Soule with ſuch delight
Who to lament erſt while was onely meet,
Doth now determine to put griefe to flight,
Being perſwaded, hereupon doth reſt,
Shee ſhall not be forſaken though diſtreſt.

Gods

Gods Favour toward me is hereby proved,
For that he hath not quite dejected me;
VVhy then, though crosses be not yet removed
Yet so seasoned with pacience they be,
As they excite me unto godlinesse,
The onely way to endlesse happinesse.

Weh earthly muckworms can in no wise know
Being of the Holy Spirit destitute,
They favour onely earthly things below;
Who shall with them of saving Grace dispute,
Shall find them capable of nothing lesse
Though Christianity they do professe.

Let Esaus porcion fall unto these men,
The Fatnesse of the Earth let them possesse
No other thing they can desire then,
Having no taste of Heavens happinesse,
They care not for Gods Countenance so bright,
Their Corn and Wine and Oyle is their delight.

To compasse this and such like is their care,
But having past the period of their dayes,
Bereft of all but miseries they are,
Their sweet delights with mortall life decayes.
But godlinesse is certain, great gain, *Tim.6.6*
Immortall blisse they have, who it retain.

They that are godly and regenerate,
Endu'd with saving Knowledg, Faith, and Love,
When they a future blisse premeditate,

Is

It doth all bitter paffion quite remove;
Though oft they feel the want of outward things
Their heavenly meditacions, comfort brings.

They never can be quite difconfolate,
  Becaufe they have the onely Comforter
  Which doth their minds alway illuminate,
   And make them fleſhly pleaſures much abhorr,
For by their inward light they plainly ſee
How vain all tranſitory pleaſures bee.

Moreover, if they be not only voyd
  Of earthly pleaſures and commodities,
  But oftentimes be greivoufly annoyd
  With fundry kinds of great Calammities,
Whether it be in Body, Goods, or Name,
With patience they undergo the fame.

And why? becauſe they know and be aware
  That all things work together for the beft,
  To them that love the Lord and called are, *Ro.* 8
  According to his purpoſe; therefore bleft   28.
Doubtleſſe they be, his knowledg that obtain,
No Loſſe may countervail their bleſſed Gain.

Which makes them neither murmor nor repine
  When God is pleaſ'd with Croſſes them to try,
  who out of darkneſſe cauſed light to ſhine, 2 *Cor*
  Can raiſe them Comfort out of Miſery   4.6.
They know right well and therefore are content
To beare with patience any Chaſtiſement.

                     This

This difference is betwixt the good and bad;
When as for sin the godly scourged are,
And godly Sorrow moves them to be sad,
These speeches or the like they will declare:
O will the Lord absent himselfe for ever?
Will he vouchsafe his mercy to me never?

What is the cause I am afflicted so?
The cause is evident I do perceive.
My Sins have drawn upon me all this woe,
The which I must confesse and also leave,
Then shall I mercy find undoubtedly, *Pro.*28.13.
And otherwise no true prosperity.

Whilst sin hath rule in me, in vain I pray,
Or if my Soule inniquity affects,
If this be true, as tis, I boldly say,   8.
The prayer of the wicked, God rejects; *Pro.*15,
If in my heart I wickednesse regard
How can I hope my prayer shall be heard. *Psal.*66

If I repent, here may I Comfort gather,
Though in my prayers there be weaknesse much
Christ siteth at the right hand of his Father
To intercede and make request for such, *Rom.*8.
Who have attained to sincerity,   33.
Though somthing hindered by infirmity.

I will forthwith abandon and repent,
Not onely palpable inniquities,
But also all alowance or consent

                                                        To

To finfull motions or infirmities;
And when my heart and wayes reformed be,
God will with-hold nothing that's good from me
Pfal. 84.

So may I with the *Pſalmiſt* truly fay,
Tis good for me that I ave been afflicted,
Before I troubled was, I went aftray, *Pfal* 119
But now to godlineffe I am adcted;
If in Gods Lawes I had not took deli-ht,
I in my troubles fhould have perifht quite.

Such gracious fpeeches ufually proceed
From fuch a Spirit that is Sanctifide,
Who ftrives to know his own defects and need
And alfo feekes to have his wants fupplide;
But certainly the wicked do not fo
As do their fpeeches and diftempers fhow.

At every croffe they murmor, vex and fret,
And in their paffion often will they fay,
How am I with Calamities befet!
I think they will mee utterly deftray,
The caufe hereof I can in no wife know
But that the *Deſtinies* will have it fo

Unfortunate am I and quite forlorn,
Oh what difaftrous Chance befalleth me!
Vnder fome hurt'full Plannet I was born
That will (I think) my Confufion be,
And there are many wickeder then I
Who never knew the like adverfity.

These words do breifly show a carnall mind
Polluted and corrupt with Ignorance,
Where godly Wisdom never yet hath shin'd
For that they talk of Destiny or Chance;
For if Gods Power never can abate,
He can dispose of that he did create

If God alone the True Almighty be
As we beleive, acknowledg, and confesse,
Then supream Governor likewise is he
Disposing all things, be they more or lesse;
The eyes of God in every place do see
The good and bad, and what their actions bee.

The thonght hereof sufficeth to abate
My heavinesse in great'st extremity,
When Grace unto my Soul did intimate
That nothing comes by Chance or Destiny,
But that my God and Saviour knowes of all
That either hath or shall to me befall

VVho can his servants from all troubles free
And would I know my Crosses all prevent,
But that he knowes them to be good for me
Therefore I am resolv'd to be content,
For though I meet with many Contradictions
Yet Grace doth alwayes sweeten my Afflictions.

FAint not my Soule, but wait thou on the-
　Though he a while his answer may suspend,
Yet know (according to his blessed word)
·He will vouchsafe refreshing in the end,
Yea though he seem for to withdraw his grace,
And doth not alwaies show his pleasing face.

　As by the Sun, though not still shining bright,
　We do enjoy no small Commodity,
　Whilst that the day is govern'd by his Light,
　And other works of Nature testify
His wonderfull and rare Effects alwayes,
Though often vayled be his shining rayes.

　So it is no small mercy, though we see
　Gods Countenance not alwaies shining bright,
　That by the same our minds enlightned be,
　And our affections guided by that Light,
And whilst the winter-fruits as it were we find
In Pacience, Sufferings, and Peace of mind.

　Then let it not be told in *Ashkelon*,
　Neither in *Gath* let it be published,
　That those that seek the Lord and him alone
　In any case should be discouraged,
Lest it rejoyce the wicked this to see,
Who think the wayes of grace unpleasant be.

　　　　　　　G　　　　　Where

Where-as they are most pleasant, sweet, and fair
Yeilding delights which onely satisfy
Our minds, which else transported are with care
And restlesse wandrings continually,
But those that do no taste hereof attain
Seek rather for content in pleasures vain.

When *Kain* had lost the happy harmony,
He by a peacefull Conscience might enjoy
His nephew *Iubal* then most skilfully
Invented Musick, thereby to convey
Unto the outward eare some melody,
But no true joy comes to the heart thereby.

For it is onely a Certificate |Grace
Brought by Gods Spirit from the Throne of
That may delight the Soule Regenerate,
Which certifies her of her happy case,
That shee's already in a gracious state,
Which will in endlesse glory consummate.

Again, the blessed Soule may take delight,
To think on Sions great prosperity,
In that the Gospell long hath shined bright,
Sustaining no Eclips by Heresy,
So that the meanes of knowledg is so free,
Gods Worship rightly may performed be.

If then my Soule, the Lord thy Portion be
Delight in his Word and sacred Covenants
Wherby his Graces are conveyed to thee,
As Earnests of divine inheritance,   And

And which may caufe tru comfort to abound
Thy Lot is fallen in a pleafant ground,

Then let not any trouble thee difmay
Seeing the Light of Grace to thee hath fhone
The fable Weed of fadneffe lay away,
And put the Garment of falvacion on.
With chearfulneffe, Goods bleffings entertain
Let not the object of thy mirth be vain,

Which as a Cloud would ftop the influence
Of that true Light that doth the Soule refine
And predi poteth it through lively fence
To that eternall brightneffe moft divine;
Then cheifly to admit that joy, accord,
Which commeth by the Favour of the Lord.

God's Favour ever highly eftimate,
As the prime motive of tru happineffe,
VVhereof, fince that thou didft participate,
In Life or Death, feare no kind of diftreffe;
VVhen humane help fha'l fayl thee utterly,
Then is Gods faving opportunity.

Deadneffe of fpirit that thou mayft avoyd,
The lively means of godlyneffe embrace,
And ceafe not feeking though thou be delayd,
But wait till God do manifeft his grace,
For thy deliverance, prefix no day,
But patiently the Lords due leifure ftay.

G 3

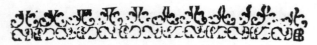

The fourth Meditacion.

ALas my Soule, oft have I fought thy Peace,
But ftill I find the contrary encreafe,
Thou being of a froward dilpoficion,
Perceiveft not thy mercyfull Phyfician   [cions
Doth give thee for hy health thefe ftrong purga-
So may we call our daily moleftacions,
VVhich how to beare, that thou mayft underftand
Take heed of two extreams under Gods hand,
The one is, too light takeing thy Diftreffe,
The other's, hopeleffe Greife or Penfiveneffe;
Between thefe two, obferve with heedfull eye
A middle courfe or mediocrity;
Confider for the firft, if one correct
His Chi'd, who feemeth it to difrefpect,
VVarding the blow or fetting light therby,
How is he beat again defervedly;
So if that thou fhould'ft feem to difregard,
The Chaftiments of God, or feek to ward
The fame by wayes or meanes impenitent,
How juft fhall God renew thy punifhment:
If Phyfick for our Bodies health be tane,
VVe hinder not the working of the fame,
Strong Phyfick if it purge not, putrifies,
And more augments then heales our malladies,
And as is fyd, our manifold Temptacions,
Are not ime but thy fcouring Purgacions,

Wherein

VVherin a dram too much, hath not admiffion,
Confeated by fo Skilfull a Phyfician
VVho will not have their bitterneffe abated,
Till thy ill humors be evacuated;
Then loofe it down for thy Humilliacion,
And hinder not its kindly Opperzcion,
As thou mayft by untimely voyding it
By vain contentments, which thou mayft admit,
VVhich makes us drive repentant thoughts away,
And fo put far from us the Evill day;
But that content which is by fuch meanes got
Is like cold water, tane in fevers hot,
VVhich for the prefent, though it feem to eafe,
Yet after it encreafeth the difeafe;
But thou doft rather unto Grief incline,
At Croffes therfore, fubject to repine,
Suppofing oft, thy prefent troubles are
Intolerable, and thy bane declare;
VVhilft thou for this, thy felfe doft maferate
Difpair unto thee doth intimate,
That none hath been afflicted like to thee,
Unparaleld thy vifitacions bee;
The by-waies being thus difcovered,
Endeavour in the right way to be led,
With tru Repentance, hope of pardon joine,
Deny thy felfe, and truft for help divine,
Seek firft with God in Chrift to be at peace,
Who onely can thy Tribulacion ceafe,
For he that laid the Rod (affliction) on,
The power hath to pull it off alone;

Twere

'Twere but in vain for one that were in debt,
To see the Officers a discharg to get,
Till with his Creditor he doth agree
He cannot walk out of his danger free;
So vain are they, which think their course is sure,
When in the use of meanes they rest secure,
Whereas if God his blessing doth restrain
VVe by the creature can no help attain:
Though it hath pleased God out of his grace,
Naturall causes over things to place.
Yet keeps he to himselfe, (blest be his name)
The state and operation of the same;
Then do not think my Soule to find redresse
By meanes of Freinds, or by self Skilfulnesse,
But rather all created helps deny,
Save as they serve for God to work thereby:
Now forasmuch as God is just alone,
Know, without cause he hath afflicted none,
Sith without doubt, his wayes so equall be,
For sem great fault he thus correcteth thee,
Therfore to lowest thoughts thy self retire,
To seek the cause that moved God to ire.
Which when thou findest, whatsoere it be
As thy right hand or eye so dear to thee,
Resolve for ever to abandon it,
Be watchfull lest the same thou recommit,
Renew thy Covenant with God, and vow
In the remainder of thy dayes, that thou
Wilt walk before him with an upright heart
If for that end his grace be on thy part,

If

If when hereto thou dost thy forces try,
In them thou find a difability,
Then look to Chrift, who doth thy weakneffe veiw
And of compaffion will thy ftrength renew,
From him alone thou mayft that grace derive
Which like a Cordial or Reftorative,
Will ftrengthen and repair thy faculties,
Which elfe are dead to holy exercife,
Twill make thy Underftanding apprehend
God as a Father, who in Love doth fend
Correction to his Children when they ftray,
When without check the wicked take their fway;
This grace once tafted, fo affects the will,
As it forfaketh that which cannot fill ;
The well of living waters, to frequent,
Can onely fill the Soule with tru content;
The memory it doth corroberate,
To keep a ftore, the Soule to animate,
Gods precious promifes the treafures be,
Which memory referves to comfort thee;
The over-flowings of this grace divine
To goodneffe the affections will encline;
Turning the hafty current of thy love
From things below, unto thofe things above,
Seeing it is the grace of Chrift alone,
Which makes the Soule to be with God at one,
Endeavour for it, give thy felfe no reft,
Till feelingly thereof thou be poffeft.

The fifth Meditacion.

SUch is the force of each created thing,
That it no solid happinesse can bring,
Which to our minds may give contentments sound
For like as *Noahs* Dove no succour found,
Till shee return'd to him that sent her out,
Just so the Soule in vain may seek about,
For rest or satisfaction any where,
Save in his presence, who hath sent her here.
Gods omnipresence I do not deny,
Yet to the Faithfull he doth spec'ally,
Alone his gracious presence evidence,
VVho seeing all true blessings flow from thence,
Are troubled onely when he hides his Face,
Desiring still to apprehend his Grace,
This Grace of God is taken diversly
And first it doth his Favour signify,
That independent Love of his so free,
Which mov'd him to his mercyfull Decree,
His *Merum beneplacitum* it is
That's motive of all good conferd on his:
The fruits of this his Love or Favour deare,
Are likewise called Graces every where,
Election and Redempcion, graces are,
And these his Favour cheifly do declare.

Faith,

Faith, Hope, Repentance, Knowledg, and the reſt,
Which do the new Creac'on manifeſt,
Now theſe are counted Grace habituall.
And laſtly, this the Grace of God we call,
His actuall Aſſiſtance on our ſide,
VVherby we overcome when we are tride;
How ever then the word is underſtood
Grace is the cheif deſirable good.
Tis *Summum bonum*; is it ſo? for why?
Becauſe without it no Proſperity,
Or earthly Honours, in the high'ſt degree,
Can make one truly happy ſayd to be,
For as we might their miſeries condole
Who ſhould inhabit neare the Northern-Pole,
Though Moon & Stars may there apear moſt bright
Yet while the Sun is abſent, ſtill tis night,
And therfore barren, cold, and comfortleſſe,
Vnfit for humane creatures to poſſeſſe:
More fruitleſſe, empty comfort is the Mind,
Who finds the Sun of Righteouſneſſe declind,
Yea, though all earthly glories ſhould unite
Their pomp and ſplendor, to give ſuch delight,
Yet could they no more ſound contentment bring
Then Star-light can make graſſe or flowers ſprings
But in that happy Soule that apprehends
His Loving kindneſſe, (which the Life tranſcends)
There is no lack of any thing that may
Felicity or tru delight convey;
As whilſt the Sun is in our Hemiſphere,
We find no want of Moon nor Star-light cleare,

So

So where the Fountain of tru Light diſplayes
H ... nes, there is no need of borrow'd joyes,
For w   . he is who made all things of nought,
T ... . p. eſence ſtill freſh joyes are wroughts
Nor ... I he ſelp to make a happy one,
Sith a perfection is in him alone,
Grant th. n hi. Grac . is moſt to be deſir'd
And nothi g elſe to be ſo much requir'd;
But here a carnall crew are to be blam'd,
By whom the Grace of God ſo much is nam.'d
Who are experienc'd in nothing leſſe
As do their courſe and practiſes expreſſe,
For though they ſay the Grace of God's worth all
Yet will they hazzard it for Trifles ſmall,
Here t they'll put you out of all ſuſpicion
VVhen Gods Grace coms with mens in competi-
For holy duties lightly ſuch neglects,   ｜cion
Whereby Gods Love is felt with its effects,
The favour of a mortall man to gain
Though but a ſhew thereof he do attain, ſ
And that perhaps for ſome employment baſe
VVhich one cannot perform and keep tru Grace,
Therefore tis probable, how ere they prate,
Gods Grace they value at too low a rate
For to be purchaſt by them, ſith they leave
Their hold of it, a ſhaddow to receave;
But they that do in truth of heart profeſſe
That they have found this Pearle of Bleſſedneſſe
Will not adventure it for any thing,
What ever good it promiſeth to bring,

Becauſe

Becaufe they know the choifeft quinteſence
Of earthly pleaſures greateſt confluence,
Cannot procure that ſweet bliſſefuil peace
Which from Gods Favour ever takes encreaſe;
Yet many times it comes to paſſe we ſee,
That thoſe who have tru grace ſo ſenſleſſe be
Of it, that they in ſeaſons of diſtreſſe,
Abundance of impacience do expreſſe,
But tis their ſin, and brings an ill report
Upon their cheifeſt Comfort, Strength and Fort;
Such therefore ſhould endeavour paciently,
To beare whatever croſſe upon them iy,
And that by ſtrength of this conſideracion
That they have need of this theyr tribulacion 1 *Pet*
It may be to mind them of ſome offence   1.6.
Which they committedhave (perhaps) long ſince
Yet they remaine unhumbled for it,
Or elce (may be) ſome Duty they omit,
In which remiſſive courſe they will remain,
Till with a Rod they be brought home againe;
Or if they would conſider how they prove
The Lords great Pacience towards them and Love
In wayting for theyr turning to his wayes,
They would not think ſo greivous ot delayes,
Of reſtitucion to that ſolace found,
VVhich in the ſence of Grace is ever found,
VVhich whoſo will in Heart and Life preſerve,
Theſe following directions muſt obſerve;
The firſt is, to purge out inniquities
VVith all that might offend Gods puer eyes,

                                              Th

(92)

The next is, to have Faith in Chrift, and Love
Of God, and that which he doth beſt approve;
Humility muſt likewiſe have a place
In them that will be ſure of tru Grace,   *Iam.4.6*
Then there muſt be ſincear Obedience
To all *Jehovah's* juſt Commandements,
For God will manifeſt himſelf to thoſe,
Who by Obedience, Love to him diſcloſe. *Ioh.14*
Now laſtly, that which fits one to embrace
The ſence of God's exceeding Love and Grace
Is ſkilfulneſſe in that moſt bleſſed Art
Of walking with the Lord with upright heart,
That is to manage all things heedfully,
As in the veiw of Gods omniſcient eye,
And ſo, by conſequence, by Faith to joyne
In union with the Trinity divine;
This is the very life of happyneſſe,
Which one may feel far better then expreſſe:
But left whilſt being wrapt above my ſphere,
With ſweetneſſe of the Theame, I ſhould appeare
Quite to forget the nature of a Song,
And to ſome this might ſeem over-long,
My thoughts theyr workings, ſpeedily ſuſpends,
And at this time my Meditacion ends.

Finis.

Verses on the twelvth Chapter
of *Ecclesiastes*.

ALl Earthly Glories to theyr periods post,
As those that do possesse them may behold,
Who therfore should not be at too much cost
With that which fades so soon, dies & growes old
    But rather minde him in their youthfull dayes,
    Who can give glory which shall last alwayes.

Ere Light of Sun or Moon or Stars expire,
Before the outward sence eclipsed be,
VVhich doth direct the heart for to admire
These works of God which obvious are to see,
    The Fabrick of the Earth, the Heavens high,
    Are to the mind discoverd by the eye.

Again, before the strong men, low shall bow,
And they that keep the house shall tremble sore
Ere natures force be spent, or quite out-flow;
And wonted courage shall be found no more,
    VVhen weaknesse shall each part emasculate
    And make the stoutest heart effeminate.

                        Moreover

Moreover, ere the grinders shall be few
VVhich for concoction doth the food prepare,
And Dames of musick shall be brought so low
That for their melody none much shall care;
    Harsh and unpleasant, then the voyce shall bee
    The breast being not from obstructions free.

Also before that, causlesse feares arise,
By reason of much imbecility,
Conceit of harmes will in the way surprise
Such feeble ones, which would from shadowes fly.
    VVhen chilling Frost of sad decrepid age,
    The force of vitall vigour shall aswage.

The Almond Tree shall blossoms then declare,
Gray hairs presage to them the end is nigh,
Naturall heat having no more repaire,
Desires sayle, as flames wanting fuell, dy,
    Nothing remayning whereby strength s suppli'd
    The marrow wasted, and the moysture dri'd.

And ere the silver cord be loose and weak,
Let be the veins be stopt, and sinews shrink
And ere the pitcher slow, or Pitcher break,
Let me the seat for water or spirit shrink
    The head whereas the animals reside,
    Now full of maladies, and stupyfide.

The Body thus out-worn and quite decayd,
The dust returneth to the Earth again;
To God who gave it, is the Soul convayd
Who doth with it as he did preordain,
   However som to vent their falacy
   Conclude the Soul doth with the Body dy.

Which if were truth why did our Saviour say?
Fear him not which the Body kils alone, *Mat* 10
And hath no might the Soul for to destray,   28.
It with the one the other must be gone;
   But that they may declare impostors skill
   Twixt Soul and Spirit they distinguish will.

The Soul (say they) doth with the Body dy,
Then there's a third part which they Spirit call,
Who doth return to God immediatly
Leaving the Dead till judgment-generall,
   And then returning breathing doth infuse
   In Soul and body, wherby life ensues.

For which they have no Scripture (I suppose)
Save what they wrest unto theyr own Perdicion,
As this, where 'tis said, the word with power goes
Twixt Soul & Spirit by divine commission *H.* 6.4.
   Twixt joynts and marow it doth penetrate, 12.
   Seeing all secrets, heart can meditate.

                           The

The joynts and marrow of the Body be
Not sev'rall specie's, but of kind the same,
The Body to support, each part agree,
And ev'ry member hath its sev'rall name;
   So Soul and Spirit is one entire thing,
   Immortall by the vertu of its Spring.

More texts of Scripture these Deceivers wrest,
Which should be answered, Truth for to defend;
But seeing here I have so long digrest,
What I begun, I hasten now to end,
   Which is to stir up youth their God to mind,
   Before effects of evill dayes they find

All here is vanity the Preacher sayes,
Yea use of many books are wearisome,
If cheifly don for self-respect or prayse
It doubtlesse will to such a snare become:
   Of all the matter, then the End let's hear,
   Keep Gods commandements with son-like fear.

FINIS.

Appendix: Difficult-to-read passages in the original

A3v, Stanza 4:

This time was when the Sonne of Righteousnesse
His Luster in the world began to spread,
Which more and more to his he doth expresse
In tearms so large that they that run may read,
And to himselfe he doth the weaker lead;
He to his bosum will his Lambs collect,
And gently those that feeble are direct. Isa. 40.11

. . .

4, Stanzas 3 and 4:

Yea like the messengers of *Iob*, they hast,
One comes before another can be gon,
All mocions of delight were soon defast,
Finding no matter for to feed upon,
They quickly were disperced every one,
Wherea<t m>y minde it self, would much torment,
Vpon t<he rac>k of restless discontent.

The summers day, though chearfull in it selfe,
Was wearisom, and tedious, unto me,
As those that comfort lack, content or health,
To credit this may soon'st perswaded be,
For by experience truth hereof they see.
Now if the summers day, cause no delight,
How irksome think you was the winters night.

. . .

5, Stanzas 2, 3 and 4:

So (to be briefe) I spent my infantcy,
And part of freshest yeares, as hath been sayd
Partaking then of nothing cheerfully
Being through frailty apt to be affraid,
And likely still distempered or dismaid,
Through present sence of some calamity,
Or preconceipt of future misery.

But as the longest winter hath an end
So did this fruitlesse discontent expire,
And God in mercy some refreshing send,
whereby I learn'd his goodnesse to admire,
And also larger blessings to desire;
For those that once, have tasted grace indeed,
Will thirst for more, and crave it till they speed.

But that I may proceed Methodicall,
When first the restlesse wanderings of my minde,
Began to settle, and resolve with all
No more to be desturb'd with every winde
It such a pleasing exercise did finde,
Which was to ponder what Worth ech day,
The sence of Heareing should to it convay.

. . .

8, Stanzas 3 and 4:
There is a kind of counterfet content,
Wherwith some are deceivd, tis to be feard,
Who think they need not sorrow, or lament,
Being to sensuall pleasures so indeard;
Whose minds are stupid, & their concience ceard
Elce might they see all Earthly delectatcion,
To be but vanity, and hearts vexacion. *Eccl.* 2.

To lightning, carnall merth we may compare,
For as a flash it hastes and soon is gon,
Foretelling of a Thunder clap of care,
It also blastes the heart it lighteth on;
Makes it to goodnesse, senceless as a ston:
Disabling every part, and faculty,
Of soul and body unto piety.

. . .

9, Stanzas 3 and 4:

Then sought I carefully to understand,
The grounds of true Religion, which impart
Divine Discreshion, which goes far beyand,
All civill policy or humane Art;
Which sacred principles I got by heart:
Which much enabled me to apprehend,
The sence of that whereto I shall attend.

First touching God, there is one God I know,
who hath his being of himself alone, *Rom*. 1.20
The fountain whence al streams of goodnesse flow
But body, parts, or passions hath he none; *Ia*. 1 7
And such a Diety, there is but one; 1 *Cor*. 8.4.
Eternal, Infinite, alone is hee, 1 *Iohn*. 5.7.
One perfect Essence, distinct Persons Three.

. . .

12, Stanza 4:

Whether in body goods or name it be,
And which is worce, the soules perplexity,
Whose conscience is awake, from deadnesse free
When she considers what felicity,
She hath exchang'd for endlesse misery;
Can but torment her selfe with bootlesse care,
Fore-see-ing that her pains eternall are.

. . .

20, Stanza 1:

The second is a vehement desire,
Or ardent longing to participate
Of Christ, and eke his benifits entire
And nothing else can this desire abate,
Consume or limit, quench or mittigate:
As doth the Hart the water brook desire,
So humble Souls a Saviour doth require.

. . .

22, Stanza 4:
Now to be justifide, is to be freed,
From gilt and punishment of sin likewise,
To be accepted as for just indeed,
With God, whose grace it is that justifies;
And not our works, as vainly some surmise:
But that we may still orderly proceed,
It followeth next how we from sin are freed.

. . .

23, Stanzas 1–3:
The sins of those that God will justifie,
Were by Christs sufferings so abolished,
As that they cannot hurt them finally,
Were they as Scarlet or the Crimson Red, *Esay*.
They shall be white as Snow and cleared, 16.16
Even by Christs Blood, the which to free was spent
The faithfull, from deserved punishment.

Now comes to be considered how they may
With God, for Perfect-just, accepted be,
Who of them-selves by nature (truth to say)
Are in no part from sinnes corruption free,
How such are tane for just, here may we see,
Christs righteousnesse is theirs, by imputacion,
And so esteem'd by gracious acceptacion.

The true beleevers benifits are great,
Which they by being justifide possesse
For such shall stand before Gods judgment seat,
As worthy of Eternall Happinesse,
Even by the merits of Christs Righteousnesse,
For of themselves, they cannot merit ought,
Who are not able to think one good thought.

. . .

54, Stanza 4:
From this our Rock proceeds likewise,
Those living streames, which graciously
Releives the soule which scorched lies,
Through sence of Gods displeasure high,
Due to her for inniquity.

. . .

On page 56 of the original text, the first letters of the first word on each line are partially cropped or difficult to read. Those words apparently are as follows:

But / such / His / And / Who //
Nor / Whose / Because / To / Whose //
But / Of / His / As / His//
Therefore / Upon / When / Thy / Whom //
THe / I / Which / With / This

. . .

58, Stanzas 3, 4, and 5:
My little Hopes of worldly Gain I fret not at,
As yet I do this Hope retain; though Spring be lat
Perhaps my Sommer-age may be,
Not prejudiciall, but benificiall
Enough for me.

Admit the worst it be not so, but stormy too,
Ile learn my selfe to undergo more then I doe
And still content my self with this
Sweet Meditacion and Contemplacion
Of heavenly blis,

Which for the Saints reserved is, who persevere
In Piety and Holynesse, and godly Feare,
The pleasures of which blis divine
Neither Logician nor Rhetorician
<Can well define.   Finis>

. . .

<u>59, Stanza 3:</u>
Calling to mind their wretchednesse
That seem to be in happy case
Having externall happinesse
But therewithall no inward grace;
Nor are their minds with knowledg pollisht
In all such vertues are abollisht

. . .

<u>61, lines 13–18:</u>
Yet none may therfore just occasion take
To shun what Vertu manifest should make,
For like the Sun shall Vertu be beheld
When Clouds of Envy shall be quite dispeld;
Though there be some of no disart at all
Who no degree in worth can lower fall,

. . .

On page 68 of the original text, the first letters of the first word on each line are partially cropped or difficult to read. Those words apparently are as follows:

They / And / The //
Such / Corrupting / He / From / Which / With / Which //
A / The / If / They / And / Which / And //
Great / To / With / And / First / They / Then //
The / With / The / And

. . .

71, Stanzas 2 and 3:

The Understanding, Will, Affections cleare,
Each part of Soule and Body instantly
Losing their purity, corrupted were
Throughout as by a loathsom Leprocy
The rayes of Vertu were extinguisht quite
And Vice usurpeth rule with force and might.

This sudden change from sanctitude to sin
Could but prognosticat a fearfull end,
Immediatly the dollour did begin,   [fend
The Curse that was pronounc'd, none might de-
Which Curse is in this life a part or some,
The fulnesse thereof in the life to come.

. . .

<83>, Stanza 1:

Then let not any trouble thee dismay
Seeing the Light of Grace to thee hath shone
The sable Weed of Sadnesse lay away,
And put the Garment of Salvacion on,
With chearfullnesse, Gods blessings entertain
Let not the object of thy mirth be vain,

. . .

90, lines 1–15:

So where the Fountain of tru Light displayes
His beames, there is no need of borrow'd joyes,
For where he is who made all things of nought,
There by his presence still fresh joyes are wrought
Nor need he help to make a happy one,
Sith all perfection is in him alone,
Grant then his Grace is most to be desir'd
And nothing else to be so much requir'd;
But here a carnall crew are to be blam'd,
By whom the Grace of God so much is nam'd
Who are experienc'd in nothing lesse
As do their course and practises expresse,
For though they say the Grace of God's worth all
Yet will they hazzard it for Trifles small,
Hereof they'll put you out of all suspicion

. . .

94, Stanzas 2 and 4:

Also before that, causlesse feares arise,
By reason of much imbecility,
Conceit of harmes will in the way surprise
Such feeble ones, which would from shadowes fly
When chilling Frost of sad decrepid age,
The force of vitall vigour shall aswage.

And ere the silver cord be loose and weak
Before the veins be stopt, and sinews shrink
And ere the golden Bowl or Pitcher break,
Before the heart for want of spirit shrink
The head whereas the animals reside,
Now full of maladies, and stupyfide.